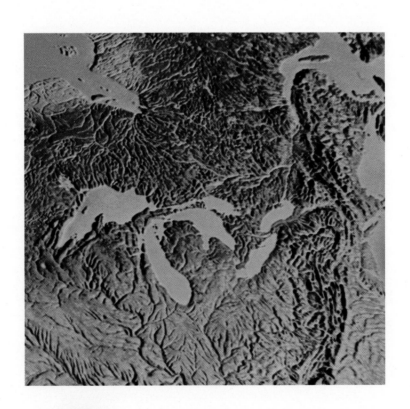

Seaway

Sunset on the Seaway.

Seaway

The Untold Story of North America's Fourth Seacoast

JACQUES LESSTRANG

A SALISBURY PRESS BOOK
A division of Superior Publishing Company
Seattle, Washington

Library of Congress Cataloging in Publication Data

LesStrang, Jacques.
Seaway.

"Salisbury Press book."
Includes index.
1. St. Lawrence Seaway. I. Title.
TC427.S3L47 386'.5 76-2471
ISBN 0-87564-216-0

FIRST EDITION

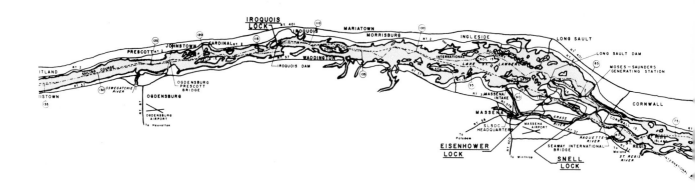

Printed and Bound in Canada by Evergreen Press, Ltd.,
Vancouver, B.C.

*This book is for the Mehaffey family
—all of them—
for what they were, and for what they did.*

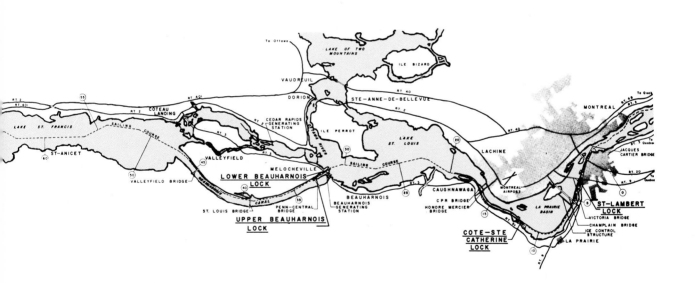

Preface

WHEN I FIRST considered doing a book on the Seaway, my objectives were threefold: to tell a story which had never been entirely told; to cause attention to be focused upon the people who have played a role in establishing the Seaway's greatness, and most particularly, to point out the unbelievable inequities placed upon the waterway—inequities which have existed since before the Seaway was born, and which still exist today.

The obligation of the Seaway to repay for its construction and the concomitant tolls system stand out as the most unjust handicap ever placed upon a transportation system. And the handicap is unique. In the long history of waterway transportation and national transportation improvements in both the United States and Canada, only upon the Seaway has such a stultifying regulation ever been placed.

In a book called The Jungle *in 1909, Upton Sinclair focused attention upon the inhumane conditions under which animals were killed at U.S. slaughterhouses, and the public displeasure that followed led to legislative action which eliminated slaughterhouse cruelty. It is my hope that the focus of this volume might have a similar effect, and that it can become a catalyst for the establishment of a fair and equal treatment for the Seaway.*

Above and beyond that, as I indicated earlier, Seaway *was meant to place in historical perspective the people who have played so vital a role in the Seaway's origins, and those others who have taken on the unrewarding role of leadership today and who continue to make its history.*

It is a well know fact that there are always a lot of people who are involved in making a book such as this one really happen. I am indebted to more of them than I could ever mention here. I am indebted to many friends in the United States and Canada who assisted with references and photographs, particularly to my good friend Stuart Abbey whose well-taken photos grace many of our pages, to Linda Marcks for so assiduously typing and retyping the manuscript, to Madelyn Pruski at the Seaway Development Corporation, to Walter Mazon, who helped so generously with research documents, and to a great many people at The White House and in both houses of Congress. They know who they are. Virtually every name the reader will come across as this volume unfolds has played a role, albeit unknowingly, in its execution, and they thusly merit our thanks.

And most of all, there must be a note of gratitude and appreciation for my own Barbara, who saw from the very first the drama in the telling of the untold story of the St. Lawrence Seaway. Her hard work and patience and, most of all, her enthusiasm played a very major role in making it all happen. J.L.

Coraledge
St. Mary's Parish
Jamaica, W.I.
and
Stone House
Little Glen Lake, Michigan

Contents

St. Lambert, first lock in the Seaway system.

1

The St. Lawrence Seaway: an Overview

The Saint Lawrence Seaway is an American legend—it is, in fact, one of the great legends of modern times. And yet, for some inexplicable reason, it never quite succeeded in achieving that popular status, that reputation for immensity of purpose or that aura of Herculean effort which is the point from which all legends must begin.

Yet, not since the building of the pyramids, has mankind conceived, let alone realized, an engineering feat of such magnitude. When it was readied for navigation in 1959, the Seaway had opened the Great Lakes to the sea, creating half-a-hundred international deep-draft ports, tying the heartland of North America to the commerce of the world, permitting ships from Casablanca and Rotterdam and Le Havre to find ports of call at Cleveland and Detroit and Duluth.

In other words, the St. Lawrence Seaway created a new coastline for the United States— a fourth coast—and for Canada, opening a bold, new chapter in the maritime history of North America.

Compared to the construction of the Seaway, the digging of the Suez Canal was certainly a lesser accomplishment, as was the building of the Panama Canal—although both have been memorialized on a much grander scale in the history and geography books of the world, as well as in the minds of virtually everyone.

Perhaps the reason for the lesser attention being paid to the greater feat rests somewhere in the troubled and bizarre circumstances under which this marvelous man-made route to the sea came to be realized, after tortured decades of battle and debate.

The geographer, looking at a geodesic globe of the world, would note that the Great Lakes of North America—the largest body of fresh water in the world—connects with the Atlantic Ocean through the St. Lawrence River at the Gulf of St. Lawrence. An economist would note, further, however, that albeit a series of small locks, the Great Lakes might as well be land-locked: In terms of world transportation economics, the Lakes were virtually non-existent. A shallow draft, plus white-water— the Lachine Rapids, the Soulanges and the swift-flowing International Rapids—made it impossible for the ocean ships which carried the commerce of the world to enter or leave the Lakes.

And so the maritime commerce that grew up in the Great Lakes was primarily regional— shipping went mostly from small lake port to small lake port, from the United States to Canada.

And so it remained during most of the 19th century.

As long ago as 1895 the United States and Canada appointed a deep-water commission to investigate the possibility of an extensive lock system to connect the lakes with the sea, and to open the St. Lawrence River for deep draft ocean vessels. But it took over half a century of debate and finally, the certainty of individual action on the part of Canada, before the great, defiant and powerful lobbies of the U.S. East Coast tidewater ports, led by the Port of New York, and the wealthy U.S. railroad and private power utility lobbies could be silenced enough to permit compromise legislation to construct the waterway.

A U.S.-Canadian treaty to develop a power dam to be called *The Moses-Saunders Power Dam and Facilities* was signed and ratified in 1950. In 1951 Canada created a St. Lawrence Seaway Authority and three years later the U.S. assembled a similar agency called the St. Lawrence Seaway Development Corporation, under legislation known as the *Wiley-Dondero Act.*

The physical task of building the Seaway was immense beyond description. Each section of the 112-mile construction site developed its own seemingly unsurmountable obstacles; at Montreal, for instance, the Jacques Cartier Bridge had to be raised 80 feet to provide a 12-foot clearance for ships. A single mile of

channel between the Lower and Upper Beauharnois locks, the shortest in the Seaway system, was dug out of a bed of hard, abrasive Potsdam sandstone which had to be blasted foot-by-foot, yard-by-yard, for a cost of $50 million for that one mile of Seaway.

After five years and the dredging of over 360 million tons of rock, after the resettlement of thousands of people, and entire towns, after changing the face of the earth and the homes and habits of thousands of its inhabitants— seven new locks and the world's largest joint power facility were completed.

Ships could enter the St. Lawrence River at Montreal, and through these gigantic new locks, along with the Welland Canal and the Sault Ste. Marie Locks, rise the height of a 60 story building, stair-stepped from the Atlantic to a fresh-water sea a full 600 feet above the ocean. And here, new international inland ports of two nations awaited them.

Ships now could travel 2,300 miles via inland waterways to the heart of a continent. Vessels could now carry grain from Duluth-Superior

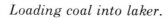

Loading coal into laker.

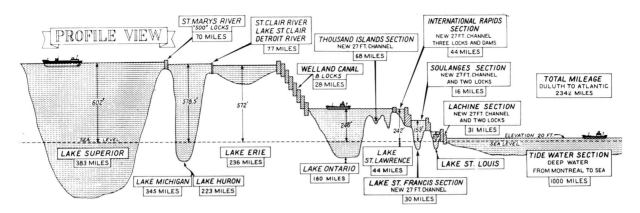

PROFILE VIEW						

Profile view of Great Lakes, showing five sections and all locks.

and the Canadian Lakehead directly overseas. Bulk carriers of the domestic Great Lakes fleet once hampered by shallow drafts could now be loaded to a draft of 25 feet, 9 inches, each ship carrying 27,000 tons—more than a million bushels of grain: the yield from more than 50,000 acres of prairie farmland.

And so the Seaway took the midsection of the continent and linked it to the world. Factors of savings of money and time and fuel became apparent now. Because most maps are Mercantor projections it was at first difficult for mariners and industry alike to recognize that the ports of the Great Lakes—Cleveland, Toledo, Buffalo, Detroit, and many others—were now actually closer to ports in the North Europe and Great Britain ranges than ports of the Atlantic seaboard.

For instance, the distance from Baltimore to Liverpool was 3,936 miles. From Detroit to Liverpool, the distance by was 236 miles less. The 236 mile difference assumed a greater importance to shippers when overland travel of 604 miles from Detroit to Baltimore was added on. So it became apparent that a savings of over 840 miles—just short of 20% of the total distance—was realized in shipping via the Seaway rather than from the tidewater port.

Today the importance of these savings can be realized when we consider that, while coastal regions are normally the dominating areas of a nation, in North America, it is the midcontinent that is economically the most important in agriculture, population, industrial production and employment. This midconti-

The Great Lakes hinterland.

Trade routes from the Great Lakes.

Almost like a modern painting, this classic view shows the bridge and unique hold configurations of the Great Lakes bulk carrier, a ship virtually unique in the maritime world.

Drawbridge opens to permit ship passage.

nent region of North America, in fact, out-produces all of the nations of the European Common Market or the whole of the Soviet Union.

Today, the agricultural and industrial greatness of the Seaway region—from the water gateway at Montreal to the lakehead ports of Superior and Michigan—is unequalled in any other area of the world. The five lakes with 95,000 square miles of navigable waters, serve some 50 ports that handle more than a million tons of cargo annually, from a tributary hinterland area of 17 states and four provinces.

As former Canadian Seaway Authority President Pierre Camu has noted, the Seaway is a great deal more than a series of gigantic steps from sea level to Lake Superior. It is a highly complex commercial system complemented by an intricate network of highway, rail and pipeline transportation links extending over more than half the North American Continent.

For most of the traffic it carries, it is a competitive rather than an exclusive route.

Ocean-going vessels bound for Great Lakes ports enter the Gulf of St. Lawrence from the Atlantic about 1,000 miles downstream from Montreal, where the Seaway begins. The waterway required no improvement to about 190 miles below Montreal. Today, Canada maintains this upstream section at a minimum depth of 35 feet. Tidal effects extend up the St. Lawrence to Trois Rivieres, about 80 miles from Montreal (see maps on pages 11 and 16).

From Montreal to Lake Ontario, the first of the five Great Lakes, the vessel rises more than 225 feet. This 182 mile stretch of waterway is comprised of five legal sections, three of which are solely in Canadian waters.

The first of these sections, some 31 miles long, enables marine traffic to bypass the Lachine Rapids. Two locks—the St. Lambert opposite Montreal, and the Cote Ste. Catherine, eight and a half miles upstream—are employed to raise vessels 50 feet to the level of Lake St. Louis, a wide section of the St. Lawrence at the confluence with the Ottawa River.

Beyond Lake St. Louis, vessels enter the second section, the Soulanges, a 16-mile stretch which includes the two Beauharnois locks, providing a total lift of about 85 feet.

The third section, 29 miles in length, terminates east of Cornwall, Ontario. It is the last of the three all-Canadian sections in the Montreal-Lake Ontario part of the Seaway.

The international segment is entered at the head of Lake St. Francis and extends to a point east of Ogdensburg, New York. Previously a swift-flowing section of the river, it was converted into a broad lake by the Moses-Saunders Power Dam which was built in conjunction with the Seaway project and lies astride the U.S.-Canadian international boundary. Owned equally by Ontario Hydro (Canada) and the Power Authority of the State of New York, this facility, with a generating capacity of some 1.8 million kilowatts, was a key factor in the construction of the Seaway.

Differences in elevation here are overcome by the United States Eisenhower and Snell locks near Massena, New York and by the Canadian control lock at Iroquois, Ontario.

The remaining 68 miles of the St. Lawrence, the Thousand Islands section, is open channel and free of rapids, although many rock shoals were removed to provide the 27 foot navigation channel.

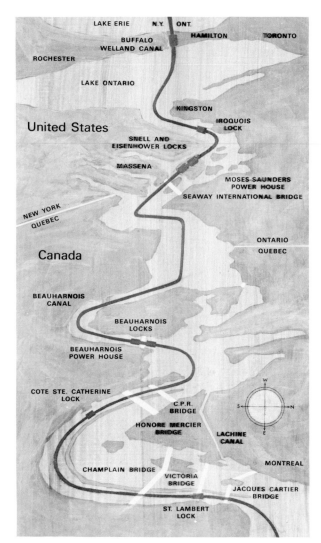

Map shows ocean-to-lakes route of the St. Lawrence Seaway.

Access to the eastern end of Lake Erie, barred by Niagrara Falls, is provided through the 27-mile Welland Canal, which has seven locks to lift vessels some 326 feet into Lake Erie.

Lakes Erie, Huron, Michigan and Superior, together with their connecting channels (The Detroit River, Lake St. Clair, the St. Clair and St. Marys Rivers, and the locks at Sault Ste. Marie) form the rest of the Great Lakes-St. Lawrence Seaway system.

So the Seaway is here today, legend or not, and it works exceedingly well for the midconti-

The twinned, stair-step locks of the Welland Canal.

nent of America, not to mention for the greater good of the entirety of both North American nations whose common boundary it has become.

Unlike the great Canadian timberlands, it has no Paul Bunyan to do it homage; nor has it the story-book heroics of a Daniel Boone, nor the romance of the great American west.

It simply is there. Doing a job for people and provinces and states and countries. And how it all happened—how the Seaway fought its way into existence, how it has had to fight furiously ever since for everything it should have been automatically entitled to, is quite a story. It's the kind of a story that, once truly told, may yet make a legend out of a ditch.

The Great Lakes as seen from Earth Resources Technology Satellite (ERTS). Storm obscures portions of Lake Superior.

A LOOK AT THE LAKES

From a geographic standpoint, the Lakes lie between latitude 41° 21′ and 49° 00′N, and longitude 76° 04′ and 92° 06′W. Lake Superior, the most northerly and westerly of the group, extends from west to east for 383 miles, from north to south for 160 miles. Lake Michigan extends for 321 miles from north to south and 118 miles from east to west, Lake Huron from northwest to southwest for 247 miles and east to west for 101 miles, and Lake Erie from east to west for 241 miles and north to south for 57 miles. The fifth lake, Ontario, extends from east to west for 193 miles and from north to south for 53 miles.

There are 7,870 miles of shore line and 95,170 square miles water surface in the Great Lakes—60,970 square miles in the United States and 34,210 square miles in Canada.

The Lakes, free of lunar tides and with only light surface currents, penetrate deep into the North American continent, forming the northeastern boundary between the United States and Canada. Two of the five largest U.S. cities with population in excess of 1,000,000—Chicago and Detroit—are located on the Lakes. Similarly, two of the largest cities in Canada, Toronto and Montreal are so located.

Lake Ontario, the most easterly of the Great Lakes and bounded on the north by the Province of Ontario and on the south by the State of New York was named by the Iroquois Indians. It is the smallest of the five lakes.

With the Welland Canal on one side and the St. Lawrence locks on the other, Lake Ontario is literally held captive by tolls. It is the only one of the Great Lakes which you can neither enter or leave without paying for the privilege.

Lake Huron, named for the Huron Indians, is the second largest of the Great Lakes. Bordered on the west by the State of Michigan, and on the north and east by the Province of Ontario, it is joined to the large Georgian Bay on the east. Lake Huron, 579 feet above sea level, covers 23,000 square miles and its greatest depth is 750 feet. It is fed from Lake Superior via the St. Marys River, from Lake Michigan and numerous streams.

Lake Erie is the second from the smallest of the Great Lakes, bordering the States of Michigan, Ohio, Pennsylvania and New York on the United States side and the Province of Ontario. Erie is the shallowest of the Great Lakes, too. It is 570 feet in (average) altitude and has a surface area of 9,930 square miles. Its maximum depth is 210 feet, with an average depth of only 58 feet. The Lake has a water volume of 109 cubic miles, a little more than one thirtieth that of Lake Superior.

Superior, the most northwesterly of the five Great Lakes, is the largest single body of fresh water in the world. Bounded on the east and north by the Province of Ontario, and on the west and south by the States of Minnesota, Wisconsin and Michigan, the Lake is feed by nearly 200 rivers.

Lake Michigan is the third largest of the great Lakes and the only one located entirely within the boundaries of the United States. It is bordered on the east and north by the State of Michigan, and on the west and southwest by Wisconsin, Illinois and Indiana. It connects with Lake Huron at the Straits of Mackinac. Lake Michigan is 579 feet above mean sea level, and covers 22,400 square miles. Its greatest depth is 923 feet.

LAKE SUPERIOR

AREA (Sq. Mi.) 31,800
COAST LINE (Miles) 1,500
LENGTH (Miles) 350
DEPTH (Feet) 1,290
WIDTH (Miles 160
ABOVE SEA LEVEL (Feet) 601.6
ABOVE LAKE ONTARIO (Feet)...........357.6

LAKE MICHIGAN

AREA (Sq. Mi.) 22,400
COAST LINE (Miles) 1,200
LENGTH (Miles) 310
DEPTH (Feet) 923
WIDTH (Miles) 118
ABOVE SEA LEVEL (Feet) 578.5
ABOVE LAKE ONTARIO (Feet)...........334.5

LAKE HURON

AREA (Sq. Mi.) 23,200
COAST LINE (Miles) 800
LENGTH (Miles) 220
DEPTH (Feet) 750
WIDTH (Miles) 100
ABOVE SEA LEVEL (Feet) 578.5
ABOVE LAKE ONTARIO (Feet)...........334.5

LAKE ERIE

AREA (Sq. Mi.) 9,932
COAST LINE (Miles) 650
LENGTH (Miles) 240
DEPTH (Feet) 210
WIDTH (Miles) 57
ABOVE SEA LEVEL (Feet) 570.5
ABOVE LAKE ONTARIO (Feet)...........326.0

LAKE ONTARIO

AREA (Sq. Mi.) 7,540
COAST LINE (Miles) 500
LENGTH (Miles) 190
DEPTH (Feet) 778
WIDTH (Miles) 55
ABOVE SEA LEVEL (Feet) 244.0

Looking aft on a laker.

2

The Political Struggles to Create the Seaway

By the end of the nineteenth century, a full third of United States tonnage shipped by water travelled between the comparatively small ports of the Great Lakes. Locks had been built at Sault Ste. Marie in 1855, and by now, the tonnage that passed through this minimum lock and canal operation—mostly bulk cargoes such as iron ore, grain and coal—doubled that of Suez. The time was right, it seemed, to talk about building a good and proper canal to put midwestern grain directly, by water, into the ports of Europe, breaking the stranglehold which the railroad monopoly had for so long held over the prairie farmer.

A Swedish immigrant from the farm districts of Minnesota, John Lind, became the first of a long, long line of legislators to introduce legislation calling for the construction of such a water route to the sea. Lind, elected to Congress by the farmers around New Ulm, Minnesota, in 1892 sponsored a congressional resolution to provide for a joint U.S.-Canadian investigation of the possibility of improving the water transportation system from "the head of Lake Superior . . . to the sea."

Two years later, in 1894, a Canadian group formed what they called a *Deep Waterways*

Association and voted their support for the Lind bi-national resolution. Even then, though, opposition to a seaway was emerging from the eastern railroads and, strangely enough, from the owners of the lake ships—water transportation interests who feared the potential competition of larger ships brought into the Lakes through an access to the sea.

Of course, improvements to the St. Lawrence had begun as far back as the beginning of the 18th century, when various small and crude locks and channels were dug. In 1834 a nine-foot channel was started at Cornwall, and similar canals were dug along the system to permit a 14-foot draft in ports of the St. Lawrence by 1908.

The success of the Lind proposal and the ultimate establishment by President Grover Cleveland of a joint U.S.-Canadian international commission to study alternatives for deep-draft ocean ships to enter the Lakes was to be the first—and for nearly half a century the last—major victory for the proponents of a seaway.

The *Deep Waterways Association* promoted similar activity in Canada where Prime Minister Mackenzie Borden supported the ac-

A U.S. Steel ore carrier along Seaway wall.
Lakers upbound and downbound.

Tunnel under Eisenhower lock permits ships to pass directly over road.

tion. So a joint U.S.-Canadian commission was formed, and before much time had passed, it had affirmed that the best route to the ocean was to seek the Canadian seaboard via the St. Lawrence River.

President Cleveland endorsed the seaway concept, and approved a series of engineering studies to deal with seaway routing. But the 19th century faded with no further direct action on the part of either the United States or Canada.

The emphasis for the St. Lawrence River during the first decade of the twentieth century seemed to deviate from navigation to power. The need for electric power to support the rapidly growing St. Lawrence region gave rise in 1906 to a Canadian public utility called Ontario Hydro. Later, a request for a public power system in upstate New York came from New York's Conference of Mayors. In the meantime, downstream, the Canadians had decided to deepen the Welland Canal to 25 feet.

Following World War I, a Duluth lawyer named Charles P. Craig convinced several Great Lakes states that they should provide delegates to form a Washington lobby to promote a seaway. *The Great Lakes-St. Lawrence Tidewater Association* emerged from the meeting of those delegates, and for sixteen years, that powerful group pushed relentlessly, if unsuccessfully, for its construction.

Further International Joint Commission studies on the St. Lawrence River were followed in 1920-21 by hearings which outlined to Congress clearly for the first time, the combined potential benefits of power and transportation to emerge from the region.

A series of battles between public and private power interests consumed most of the next decade. New York Governor Franklin Roosevelt, while not opposed to using the St. Lawrence for navigation purposes, was much more in favor of power development for the river. Largely through the efforts of a young Congressman, Bertrand Snell, from upstate New York and St. Lawrence County Republican Chairman Harry Ingram, the Power Authority of The State of New York was created, authorized to develop St. Lawrence power and to cooperate with the federal government in improving navigation on the river.

The development of an organization to deal with hydroelectric power was considered a victory for the proponents of the Seaway.

Dean Acheson, then U.S. Under Secretary of State, pointing to annual capacity of the 2,200,-000 HP to be shared equally by the U.S. and Canada, cited the economic value of the proposed Seaway project as rivaling the giant Tennessee Valley Authority (TVA) and the Panama Canal combined.

"From the standpoint of power alone," he said, "there are only eight countries in the world that produce more electricity than will be produced by the St. Lawrence Seaway and Power Project."

The United States now seemed eager to plan construction of the St. Lawrence Seaway. But Canada seemed unwilling to proceed. Canadian Prime Minister McKenzie King was able to create delay after delay in discussions relating to the physical construction of the waterway until in 1930 the unresolved Seaway

Ocean-going "salties" awaiting transit through the Welland Canal.

was one of the major issues which caused him to lose the national election.

Within two years, the new Prime Minister, R. B. Bennett and President Herbert Hoover had come to grips with the Seaway issue, and a treaty was signed by the two heads of state—a treaty to build a Seaway to a draft of 27 feet, making the U.S. responsible for completing work from Lake Superior to Lake Erie, Canada to be in charge of work in its national section, with both nations to share in the work and cost for the International Rapids section of the river. Under the treaty, costs for work already accomplished would be shared equally.

Opposition to the Hoover-Bennett Treaty was strong, immediate and vocal: The railroads again, fearing the Seaway as a competitor, denounced the treaty. The strong railroad unions—the Brotherhoods—had joined their employers in opposing the Seaway and as well, privately owned utilities, coal, Eastern and Gulf port interests, regional waterway and lake carrier organizations had joined forces to oppose the Seaway. The monstrous physical size and the combined financial strength of these self-interest factions, coupled with their unrelentless attacks upon the treaty, began at once to badly hurt its chances for survival.

Ship laden with cargo edges into a Seaway lock.

The Great Lakes port of Chicago joined forces with New Orleans against the Seaway in a *Mississippi Waterway Association*. The Lake carrier and railroad center of Cleveland, Ohio, another Great Lakes port, struck out against the Seaway. And there were others in the Lakes who did not want a route to the sea—like Toledo and Buffalo.

The Hoover-Bennett Treaty did not come up for ratification by Congress before the 1932 elections, and, of course, by then the nation was gripped in the terror of the great depression.

It was not until the 30's had passed from view that truly strong interest in the Seaway presented itself once more. It was in 1940, in fact, that President Franklin D. Roosevelt, in a statement to a Great Lakes Seaway and Power Conference said that a seaway up the St. Lawrence River "along with its benefits to national defense, will contribute to the peacetime welfare of a multitude of laborers, small businessmen, home owners and farmers . . . Such a development as we propose to carry out in the Great Lakes-St. Lawrence Basin unquestionably will result in greater activity for all ports and transportation agencies. This has been the history of all new navigation projects, and improvements directed to better commercial communication in this country and throughout the world. The fear that the Seaway will result in injury on the lower Mississippi or to our Atlantic ports is groundless."

And in a personal message to Canada's Prime Minister McKenzie King, less than a year later, FDR noted, "I am convinced of the urgent need for the large increment in low cost electric power which the St. Lawrence project will provide. Already the demand for power is running ahead of expectations. In fact, one of the most serious handicaps to the rapid expansion of U.S. airplane production is the difficulty

Dusk on Lake Erie.

of finding the large supplies of high-load factor power required for aluminum production.

"The St. Lawrence project offers by far the soundest and most economical provision for the power requirements of certain portions of our long range defense program, more particularly for certain high-load factor defense industries."

The Chamber of Commerce of the United States objected to the Seaway, saying, "It is obvious that the St. Lawrence power project cannot be justified, either in Canada or the United States, for electric power for defense industries. It would be unwise at this time, when the country is faced with the necessity of heavy outlays for national defense to divert capital, manpower, engineering talent, construction and manufacturing equipment, to projects undertaken ostensibly for national defense that cannot afford effective means of meeting present national defense requirements."

"I am convinced," Roosevelt told MacKenzie King, "that the opening of the St. Lawrence deep waterway to afford an outlet for naval and cargo ships constructed in Great Lakes shipyards, far from representing a diversion of funds and resources from the defense effort, would have the opposite effect. Our shipbuilding program, to meet the requirements of defense, will call for a great expansion of shipyards with their associated machine ships and adequate supplies of skilled labor.

"I know of no single project of this nature more important to this country's future in peace or war. Its authorization will demonstrate to the enemies of democracy that, however long the effort, we intend to outstrip them in the race of production. In the modern world that race determines the rise and fall of nations."

On June 18, 1941, Frank Knox, Secretary of the Navy, told a Congressional committee, "We are going to live in a disturbed world for a long time, no matter what the outcome of the war may be, and in that world which is out of balance and struggling for a new and secure footing, the control of the seas is going to be of immense importance."

That same year, a federal study reported that "Great Lakes shipbuilding facilities contributed substantially to the shipbuilding program of the first World War. They can now contribute equally well by assuming the burden of the small-boat program of the United States Navy, and by constructing small cargo vessels for the Maritime Commission. When completion of the St. Lawrence Seaway is within sight, then it will be possible to transfer some of the large naval shipbuilding program to the Great Lakes . . . freeing coastal yards for immediate utilization. At the same time a large merchant shipbuilding program can be initiated, thereby augmenting the shipbuilding capacity of the country by 750,000 or 1,000,000 gross tons a year."

But, Donald D. Conn, Executive Vice President of the Transportation Association of America, objected to the Seaway and the Hoover-Bennett Treaty, citing that, "No matter how vile the odor of the Illinois Waterway might become at Joliet, or what epidemics might break out, Congress could not authorize an increased diversion of water without it being subject to veto by the international tribunal (IJC)."

H. L. Bodman, representing the New York Produce Exchange before a Congressional committee on July 14, 1941, noted that ". . . we must not forget that now we have an excess of transportation." Other dissenters spoke up. The Niagara Frontier Planning Board (Buffalo) probably expressed the greatest all-around argument against the Seaway, finding virtually everything wrong with it: "The minimum total cost of the whole St. Lawrence project for both the United States and Canada would be $1,120,588,000," their report stated.

Seaway float appears in Eisenhower Inauguration Parade.

"At least 85% of the United States share of the project's cost would be borne by American taxpayers who would be the victims of unfair discrimination: These taxpayers live in the region which could not be benefitted by the St. Lawrence Seaway even if claims of proponent were valid.

"American labor, transportation and industry, on the government's estimates of probable seaway traffic, would lose $109,-647,000 a year. Diversion of business from American transportation systems to foreign carriers, diversion of Canadian export grain movement from the United States and loss to American coal producers account for this figure.

"The net loss to the United States would be $75,595,000 each year on the basis of the government's estimates of Seaway traffic. This sum represents the difference between two factors—one is the loss to established American commerce and industry plus the expense to American taxpayers; the other is the possible rate saving by shipping via the St. Lawrence.

"The American farmer would not gain from the St. Lawrence Seaway; export grain would be the chief American agricultural product to be shipped through the waterway. Even if a possible maximum saving of 3 cents a bushel were realized, this would be absorbed by the foreign purchaser and vessel owner.

"American manufacturers, who have cultivated this country's great inland market, would be seriously damaged by foreign competition resulting from the St. Lawrence Seaway: Alien tramp steamers would dump cheaply produced commodities on this currently protected Great Lakes market.

"No route for more profitable trade between American ports would be offered by the St. Lawrence Seaway: The location of the St.

Lawrence is such that no appreciable coastal or intercoastal commerce would occur.

"The St. Lawrence Seaway would not carry the volume of traffic nor bring the savings in shipping rates to the exaggerated degree cited by many proponents: They have set the probable tonnage at 11,496,000 and the probable savings at $45,516,000 annually. The more accurate estimate is $3,873,000 for tonnage and $8,822,000 for savings.

"Maintenance of wholly cordial relations between the United States and Canada might be endangered by the St. Lawrence Seaway: Serious questions could arise as to responsibility for defense of the waterway in times of war and as to preservation of water levels in Canadian harbors on the lower St. Lawrence River.

"Surrender of United States sovereignty over Lake Michigan would result from any treaty which, like the proposed treaty of 1938, limited the withdrawal of water from the lake at Chicago: It would prevent further develop-

An ore carrier moves past sister ships laid up for winter.

Vessel pulls into lock at low water, upbound for the Great Lakes, while another at high water, at the opposite gate, awaits its turn to transit downbound.

ment of the Great Lakes-Gulf of Mexico waterway by the United States.

"The United States would subsidize Canadian power to the extent of $48,860,000: This figure is reached by taking the minimum cost ($90,000,000) for the Canadian share of the power, under the least expensive plan yet advanced, and deducting costs strictly chargeable to power ($41,140,000), under the present plan.

"Whatever power benefits might result from the St. Lawrence project would affect only the State of New York and Eastern Canada: The St. Lawrence plan does not envision sale of United States power beyond the confines of New York State.

"Previous estimates of increased power demand in New York State are too optimistic: The Niagara Frontier Planning Board finds that the demand in 1952 probably will not exceed 21,000,000,000 Kilowatt-hours.

"Adequate and economical power potentialities, apart from the St. Lawrence River, exist today in New York State and Eastern Canada: Two outstanding examples are the Ottawa River in Canada and Niagara Falls."

R. V. Fletcher, General Counsel of the Association of American Railroads addressing the Atlantic States Shippers' Advisory Board, New York, January 9, 1941, thundered that ". . . railroads—management, and workers alike— in wholehearted fashion and without mental or other reservations, unanimously raise their voices in opposition to the badly conceived (Seaway) enterprise. In doing so, they join with the coal interests, both labor and capital, with the maritime interests on the Atlantic, the Gulf of Mexico, the Great Lakes and other important bodies of thoughtful and patriotic citizens, who have examined this proposal carefully and have concluded that it is fraught with injurious consequences to the public welfare."

More negative forces spoke: The New Orleans City-Wide Committee and the Mississippi Valley Association testified with great

Cranes load cargo from busy Detroit Harbor Terminal. Virtually every kind of general cargo, including containers, can be seen in the terminal yard, one of four which serve the Port of Detroit.

apparent wisdom and with an abundant knowledge of the Great Lakes that, "There is no lack of hydroelectric power available in the Great Lakes region . . . For emergency defense purposes steam power can be provided very much more quickly and eminent authorities say, at less cost than anything the St. Lawrence development can produce.

"Careful study shows that ocean navigation on regular schedules cannot be economically adapted to the Great Lakes and that the transportation benefits claimed by its proponents for the St. Lawrence project will not be realized.

"The (Hoover-Bennett) treaty would internationalize Lake Michigan, a wholly American body of water." Dr. Lewis Haney, an economist for the Mississippi Valley interests said, "Not a single skilled laborer or an hour's time of managerial or engineering skill should be wasted in the St. Lawrence River.

"The operation of the seaway will result in the loss of a coal market for American coal mines amounting to 17,000,000 tons annually— a very serious matter for American labor. It will admit cheap foreign coal into the Great Lakes region."

It was not until 1943 that the Senate actually turned its active attention to the Hoover-Bennett Treaty. Craig and his *Tidewater Association* fought furiously for it. But by a vote of 46 yea and 42 nay, failing the two-thirds majority required by law to approve a treaty, the measure failed. The Senate votes against the Seaway had been regional, of course, coming largely out of the Mississippi Valley, and from the East and Gulf coast regions: The geographic financial centers of strong tidewater and private utility lobbies and the interlock of the forces of railroads, unions, private power and financial interests.

President Roosevelt, however, at a White House press conference held on the day of the vote—March 14, 1943—said that, "Whether the thing goes through this afternoon or not makes

Left to right (standing) Kenneth M. Lloyd, M. W. Oettershagen, Edward J. Noble, Hugh Moore, Julius Cahn, Harry C. Brockel, John C. Beukema. Seated: Lewis G. Castle and Senator Alexander Wiley. (Photo taken December, 1954)

no difference at all. The St. Lawrence Seaway is going to be built, just as sure as God made green apples . . ."

Still, the defeat of the Hoover-Bennett treaty was a severe blow for the U.S. and Canadian interests which had supported the Seaway. Every Canadian Minister since 1913 had encouraged the construction of the Seaway: Borden, Meignen, King and Bennett—as had all Presidents since 1911—Taft, Wilson, Harding, Coolidge, Hoover and Roosevelt. And yet the self-interest groups, manipulating the dual levers of power and fear had successfully created continuing opposition to kill the effort. Private business, big business had demonstrated that its will was more potent than either the will of the people or the strength of government itself.

And there the matter rested until the second half of the century, when, as luck would have it

for Seaway supporters, great new iron ore fields were discovered in the Labrador wilderness— an iron strike comparable to the discovery of the great Mesabi Range. These rich ore fields required only a transportation system to get the ore out of the vast wilderness, and so a railroad was planned to carry it out, over 350 miles—to the St. Lawrence River.

By now, the once-mighty *Tidewater Association* was dead. A weak and inefficient group known as the *National St. Lawrence Association* was doing what it could to keep the Seaway concept alive. Its director, an energetic self-made man, Julius Barnes, and Dr. N. R. Danielian, decided that now was the opportune time to restructure and reorganize the Association into the kind of strong fighting force that the *Tidewater Association* had been under Charles Craig.

And that they did. Bringing power interests

into the group, Barnes almost single handedly molded a new *Great Lakes-St. Lawrence Association,* with a Duluth banker, Lewis Castle, as its executive committee chairman, and Danielian as executive vice president. By 1951 the association boasted a staff of 12, and by then, the fiery Danielian had become both the heart and the brains of the group.

The Department of Commerce had estimated that the cost of the Seaway project would be $803 million, of which the U.S. share would be $573 million and the Canadian share, $230 million. Including expenditures to date, the Corps of Engineers reported cost levels would reach $996 million inasmuch as Canada had already spent $132 million and the U. S. $32 million on various existing works related to the project.

In testimony presented before the Senate Subcommittee on the Seaway Project, it was indicated that the International Rapids section project alone would create a lot of new jobs. The estimated man hours of employment during the construction phase looked something like this:

	At Site	Off Site
Skilled labor	36,270,000	46,415,000
Semiskilled labor	13,774,000	60,717,000
Unskilled labor	32,495,000	33,093,000
TOTAL	82,476,000	140,115,000

Stability of employment in the iron and steel industry was also cited by Commerce as a labor benefit arising out of the Seaway project, along with the full development of labor in the New England region, resulting from the combination of lower-cost transportation and cheap electric power.

A second piece of good fortune for the Seaway came with the Labrador strike: Steel companies (and the lake ships which they owned) now saw, arising out of the transport of Labrador iron ore, a very strong personal profit in the construction of the Seaway. The St. Lawrence waterway suddenly became to steel interests, the logical way to carry the ore from the Labrador wilderness to their mills. And so, steel became a contributor to the Barnes' and

Danielian's new Association, supported it— and with this support, caused a major division within the here-to-fore staunchly anti-Seaway Lake Carriers Association.

The fact of increased up-bound cargoes of iron ore to balance the down-bound cargoes of grain also helped to justify the Seaway. Militarily, too, a submarine-free access from ore field to mill was cited as being substantially in the best interests of the national defense. A lot of people now, as a result of the Labrador ore strike, were beginning to pay close, positive attention to the Seaway.

Now, suddenly, things were looking up.

The importance of the St. Lawrence Seaway and Power Project to national security was outlined in a document prepared by the National Security Resources Board, covering such areas as power, the safe transport of iron ore, and shipyard availability.

"If the Seaway is not built," the 1950 report stated, "a delay of at least 18 months or more after the outbreak of war probably would be needed to produce a dependable route for moving the large amount of ore vitally needed for war production. The Seaway route is capable of being more thoroughly, easily and cheaply protected than alternate routes involving long stretches of open ocean . . ."

Speaking of the national security advantages of a St. Lawrence Valley power project, the report noted, "Because a project of such magnitude could not be initiated and carried through in the midst of a war, the national security advantages cannot be attained unless the project is well toward completion prior to any outbreak of war. Therefore, a prudent regard for national security requires that the power phase as well as the transportation phase of the St. Lawrence project be authorized now and that construction be initiated promptly."

It was Canadian Prime Minister Louis St. Laurent who provided the next impetus for Seaway construction. Now tired of delays that were U.S.-instigated (an ironic change of events, many noted), Canada decided it would

Secretary of the Army Wilbur M. Brucker (seated), Department of Defense Representative of the St. Lawrence Seaway Development Corporation in October, 1955 meets for the first time with the Corporation Officers and Members of the Advisory Board, at the Pentagon, Washington, D. C. (L to R) E. Reece Harrill, Comptroller, SLSDC; Frank G. Millard, General Counsel, Office of the Secretary of the Army; George J. Haering, Special Assistant to Administrator, SLSDC; Guerin Todd, Legal Counsel, Office of the Secretary of the Army; Lucius M. Hale, Resident Engineer, Massena Field Office, SLSDC; Raymond F. Stellar, Engineer, SLSDC; Edward R. Place, Director of Information, SLSDC; Kenneth M. Lloyd, Advisory Board, SLSDC; Hugh Moore, Advisory Board, SLSDC; Lewis G. Castle, Administrator, SLSDC; Martin W. Oettershagen, Deputy Administrator, SLSDC; John C. Beukema, Advisory Board, SLSDC; Edward J. Noble, Advisory Board, SLSDC; Harry C. Brockel, Advisory Board, SLSDC; Richard A. Hertzler, Chief, Civil Functions, Civil Military Affairs.

no longer countenance further American foot-dragging. It announced that Canada was planning to build its own all-Canada Seaway.

The U.S. began to show concern. Antagonistic forces said Canada was bluffing, that it would not, could not expend the manpower or the resources to construct the waterway alone. A new Seaway bill was introduced in Congress in 1951, but was tabled by the House Public Works Committee by a vote of 15 to 12. Following this latest U.S. legislative defeat, Prime Minister St. Laurent came to Washington to seek President Truman's support for the all-Canadian Seaway. It was no bluff. Canada was moving ahead on her own.

While Harry Truman wanted U.S. participation in the Seaway, he nonetheless reluctantly agreed to help St. Laurent by approving American participation in the power aspect of the Canadian project. A Canadian Seaway was better than no Seaway at all, *the man from Missouri* reasoned.

The Canadians moved quickly now. The St. Lawrence Seaway Authority was created by Parliament and empowered—either on its own, or in cooperation with the United States—to build a Seaway from Montreal to Lake Erie.

A new fear stirred in Washington. Seaway proponents in the United States, feeling with Truman that a Canadian Seaway was better

Sure course on a calm sea.

Bridge of a Great Lakes icebreaker.

President Richard Nixon at 10th Anniversary of the St. Lawrence Seaway.

President Gerald Ford looks over a Finnish icebreaker. His Secretary of State, Henry Kissinger, is at right.

Dusk gathers along the Seaway.

than no Seaway at all, threw their weight toward the Canadian venture. Congress became alarmed, realizing that tolls paid by American shippers for use of the Seaway would cover most of the cost, but that Canada would control and own the Seaway—an access into the heart of the American nation.

Chief spokesman for the Seaway in the House of Representatives had been John A. Blatnik, a Democrat-farm-labor Congressman from Duluth. Coming to the Congress in 1947 with strong ideas regarding the Seaway, Blatnik had back then introduced H. J. Res. 132, calling for the construction of the Seaway, thus joining the decades-long fight for a St. Lawrence waterway.

Over the next seven years, he improved and refined his legislation, and by the time of the Truman Administration, Blatnik had risen to become Chairman of the powerful House Public Works Committee—a position from which he could push the Seaway legislation.

Blatnik, after St. Laurent came to see Truman on Canada's Seaway effort, by virtue of his strength of will and personality alone, brought the Seaway measure back for consideration in Congress.

General Lewis Pick, Chief of the Army Corps of Engineers had by now given his full support to the measure as had John D. Small, Chairman of the powerful U. S. Munitions Board.

Truman went to work again, telling Congress (January 28, 1952) that the question before it was "no longer whether the St. Lawrence Seaway should be built. The question before Congress now," Truman said, "is whether the United States shall participate in its construction and thus maintain joint operation and control . . . It is obviously of great significance for us to have an equal voice with Canada . . .

"In the event the United States does not elect to proceed with joint completion of the Seaway, Canada's Seaway Authority is to construct all the navigation works required to complete the Seaway from Lake Erie to Montreal . . .

". . . It seems inconceivable to me," Truman said, "that the Congress should allow any local or special interest to divest our country of its

Rep. Blatnik (right) is shown here with Mr. Lewis G. Castle, Administrator of the St. Lawrence Seaway Development Corporation. Blatnik is holding the pen used by President Eisenhower when he signed the bill authorizing the channel project into law.

Seal of the U.S. St. Lawrence Seaway Development Corporation.

Seal of the Canadian St. Lawrence Seaway Authority.

A young Rep. Blatnik talks with officials at ceremonies marking the opening of the U.S. locks of the St. Lawrence Seaway on July 2, 1958. At left is Lewis G. Castle, first U.S. Seaway Corporation Administrator.

rightful place in the joint development of the St. Lawrence River in the interest of all the people of the United States."

Representative Blatnik in a stirring speech before the House in support of the project said, "It is obvious that since the decision on whether or not we will have a Seaway has already been made, it is just a question of whether the United States shall play the dog in the manger by refusing to become a partner in this joint undertaking, or whether we shall accept our obligation to our own people and to our friendly ally to the north, Canada, by joining in the construction.

"A bottleneck has been right here in the Congress," Blatnik said, "where for too long there has been a tendency to listen to the siren song of certain selfish vested interests—the Eastern railroads, the coal interest, the private utility lobby and some Eastern and Gulf port cities—who have opposed it on the grounds that it might affect their own interests."

In June, 1952, by a vote of 43 to 40, the Senate killed the Seaway bill.

Once again the grinding, self-serving interests of rail, private utility, East and Gulf port and coal overpowered the government.

A Canadian Seaway it was to be.

The Canadian prime minister returned to Washington once again to help develop the joint U.S.-Canadian power aspect of the project. The IJC gave its blessing for a power project at Long Sault, Ont., but the Federal Power Commission, assiduously aware of the mood of the Congress in terms of appropriating money for such an effort, assisted the Port Authority of the State of New York (PASNY) to become the agency designated to fulfill the U.S. part of the power project. Even this effort ran into legal battles and appeals, much to the consternation of the Canadians, who waited impatiently to build their Seaway.

The delay ultimately saved the day for the Seaway as we know it now. Dwight Eisenhower came into office.

Not at first, but eventually he supported U.S. participation in the Seaway, and in the U.S. Senate, Senator Alexander Wiley (D. Wisc.) and in the House, Congressman George A Dondero (R. Mich.) introduced virtually identical legislation stating that the U.S. would share in the construction of the international section of the Seaway.

Congress also acted to create the St. Lawrence Seaway Development Corporation to oversee construction of the U.S. portions of the Seaway—a counterpart to the existing Canadian St. Lawrence Seaway Authority. Lewis Castle, executive vice president of the *Great Lakes-St. Lawrence Seaway Association,* was named to serve as Administrator for the newly formed SLSDC, following in the footsteps of Canada, which had named Lionel Chevrier, as Administrator for the Canadian Seaway Authority.

By a series of maneuvers initiated by Danelian and Harry Brockel, then-director of the Port of Milwaukee, the Wiley bill was constructed in such a way that it ignored the costs of channel dredging and, with an IJC decision to shift $100 million of the total Seaway cost over from navigation to power, the U.S. share of the Seaway bill came in at just $88 million. It looked like a pretty cheap way to get involved.

Maj. Gen. Bernard L. Robinson, Deputy Chief of Engineers, United States Army, told Blatnik's House Public Works Committee on June 1953, that "The Dondero Bill provides for imposition of tolls to liquidate the United States cost of participating in the St. Lawrence River Seaway. The costs to be covered include the full costs; namely, charges for interest, amortization, maintenance, operation, and repairs. Under the Canadian authorizing legislation of 1951, the Canadian Government likewise contemplates corresponding liquidation of its Seaway costs . . .

"In response to a question during the recent Senate Committee hearings, a representative of the Chicago Association of Commerce and Industry said his organization believes that every waterway should pay for itself through a user charge. Our traditional American policy, expressed by Acts of 1884 and 1909, *has been one of freedom of tolls on our inland waterways.* Waterborne commerce between the several states produces widespread benefits, and it has been our practice to cover the costs of these navigational facilities by general taxation. In no case should (all this) be construed as implying any approval on my part of the extension of the tolls concept into the Great Lakes System or to our inland waterways generally.

" . . . Mr. Chairman," Gen. Robinson concluded, "the St. Lawrence Seaway with a 27-foot channel depth will contribute greatly to our national security, as well as to our peace-time economy. It is economically justified by a wide margin on the basis of sound estimates of cost. It will be a self-liquidating project, paying its own way without placing a burden on our taxpayers. Moreover, it is a project that will be built by Canada alone if we fail to take advantage of this last opportunity to participate in its construction. Such unilateral action would not be in the best interests of this nation from either defense or commercial consideration. I therefore urge in the strongest possible terms that the Congress authorize United States participation with Canada in this improvement, so vital to the welfare of our nation."

That same week, the Committee heard A. M. Richards, Vice President, Republic Steel Corporation:

"The St. Lawrence Waterway project has shown amazing vitality over several decades. After round upon round of defeat in the Congress, each time it has reappeared with renewed vigor. It must have something to cause every President of the United States since Harding, both Democrat and Republican, including men with widely different philosophies and temper-

Executive heads of United States and Canadian Government agencies constructing the St. Lawrence Seaway. Left to right: Martin W. Oettershagen, Deputy Administrator, and Lewis G. Castle, Administrator of the St. Lawrence Seaway Development Corporation (US); Lionel Chevrier, President, and Charles Gavsie, Vice President, The St. Lawrence Seaway Authority (Canada).

US Seaway Administrator Lewis G. Castle points out to Lionel Chevrier, President of the St. Lawrence Seaway Authority of Canada an artist's sketch of the US Seaway group's proposed administration building to be located at Massena, N.Y. This 1955 photo was taken at a meeting of US and Canadian entities at the Pentagon.

ment; that is, Harding: Coolidge, who watched every penny: Hoover, the trained engineer; Franklin Roosevelt; Truman and finally Eisenhower to advocate it. Speak of their frailities as we will, yet after all, these men were put in that high position to do that which was, in their opinion, for the best interests of our country. It is inconceivable that this long, unbroken line of presidents, from both parties, all could be wrong in their consistent advocacy of the St. Lawrence Waterway.

"In short, we believe the President Eisenhower and his cabinet are right in their determination that the proposed United States participation in this project will advance the economic interests of this country as a whole; and when President Eisenhower and the National Security Council and the Joint Chiefs of Staff say, as they have, that such American participation will advance the security interests of this country, they should know what they are talking about. In our opinion the opponents of this project take an untenable position with pretensions to superior knowledge and judgment in the field.

"For ourselves, and we suspect we are not peculiar in this, we prefer the experience and the proved capacity of those to whom the defense leadership of this country has been entrusted ."

Gregory S. Prince, General Solicitor, Association of American Railroads, spoke again in angry opposition to the Seaway legislation— "The evidence is clear and convincing that a 27-foot canal is already an obsolete and outmoded waterway for ocean going vessels. That limited depth makes the 'Seaway,' the name by which this project has been affectionately and almost reverently designated by proponents through the years, one of the greatest misnomers of all time. The words should be known as the *Lake Extension canals.*

Congressional investigation revealed the degree to which the railroads had worked to control the processes of government:

A letter from R. V. Fletcher, Vice President of the Association of American Railroads to E. E. McInnis, General Counsel, Atchison, Topeka and Santa Fe Railroad Co., disclosed that, "All of us have long recognized that the only effective way to influence Congressional action is to convince the influential men in each Congressional District that the public interest and the interest of the railroads coincide.

" . . . I have the impression that most of the Congressmen, particularly those living in the smaller states and in rural districts, depend for their support upon a comparatively few men in each county in their respective Congressional districts. If we could reach the men upon whom the Congressman depends for advice and assistance in his political campaign, we would go far toward having the problem solved."

Fletcher proposed that state associations prepare mailing lists naming these influential citizens—the men behind the Congressmen.

A senate committee on Interstate Commerce noted that Fletcher asked each railroad State Association to provide him with a complete dossier on each Member of Congress and Senator, including "who he is, where he lives, what profession he follows, what is his social and political background, and particularly who are his friends, advisors and sponsors in each of the counties in his Congressional district.

"I am seeking to assemble here (in Washington) a very complete record of each Member of Congress with particular reference to the influences which control him and the persons on whom he relies for support.

"It frequently happens that a particular Congressmen occupies a key position in connection with some measure pending in Congress. if at that time we would call upon a hundred of his influential constituents in his Congressional district and persuade these persons to write or wire him their sincere conviction on the question, I think the influence would be almost immediately felt."

J. J. Pelley, President of the AAR wrote to M. W. Clement, President of the Pennsylvania Railroad that " . . . we will soon have a mailing list of approximately 75,000 influential citizens to whom material of this kind can be sent."

President Harry S. Truman holds a conference at the White House January 26, 1948, where he urged early hearings on legislation to permit a start on a proposed St. Lawrence Seaway project so an emergency supply of iron ore may be moved for the defense efforts. Left to right around table are Sen. Tom Connally (D.-Tex); Sen. Alexander Wiley (R.-Wis); Charles Wilson, defense mobilizer; John Blatnik (D.-Minn); Assistant Secretary of Commerce Thomas W. S. Davis; Maj. Gen. Lewis A. Pick, U.S. Army chief of engineers; Sen. Theodore Green (D.-RI); Charles Murphy, Counsel to the president; Secretary of the Interior Oscar Chapman; President Truman; Rep. George Dondero (R.-Mich.); Rep. Charles A. Buckley (D.-NY).

" . . . the conclusion to be drawn from the evidence on this point is so clear and unmistakable that one cannot help but wonder why the proponents have not sought authority to construct a 35-foot channel in the first instance. I believe the answer to this is clear. While, from the standpoint of the physical and functional aspects of this waterway, looked at from the viewpoint of United States interests, nothing less than a 35-foot depth makes any sense at all, proponents have realized that it would be impossible for them to justify economically the enormously increased costs of a waterway of such depth.

"Therefore they are following the age-old strategem of getting the nose of the camel under the tent by trying to get the United States to embark in the first instance upon a project of 27-foot depth."

In April, 1953, President Eisenhower wrote Senator Wiley that, "At my request, the National Security Council has considered the national security interests in the St. Lawrence-Great Lakes Seaway Project. The Council has advised me:

"1. Early initiation and completion of the St. Lawrence-Great Lakes Seaway is in the interest of national security.

"2. The United States should promptly take whatever action may be appropriate to clear the way for commencement of the project, whether by Canada alone, or, as may be later developed, by Canada and the United States jointly.

"3. It is desirable that the United States participate in the construction of the Seaway; the extent of and limitations upon such participation to be the subject of separate determination by authority other than the Council.

"The Council's findings and recommendations have my approval," Eisenhower said, "and I propose now to discuss with the Cabinet

President Dwight D. Eisenhower signs the Seaway into existence.

the extent of and limitations upon United States participation in the project."

There were always arguments—endless, protracted arguments by the vested interests.

Countering the national defense discussions, the powerful Chicago Association of Commerce and Industry stated that the Great Lakes-St. Lawrence Seaway and Power Project was, indeed, not necessary at all in the interest of national defense and might actually be injurious to American defense efforts.

It pointed to the facts that (1) Lake Superior district resources of iron ore are "sufficient to supply Great Lakes steel producing plants far into the future", (2) that eastern steel producing areas could "more effectively use imported ore," that (3) the Seaway would not be needed for that purpose at all. The Chicago group also noted that there was no need for the movement of ships into or out of the Great Lakes for construction or repair . . . no need to expand shipbuilding facilities when there were ample facilities at tidewater ship yards . . . the power phase of project would make only a minor addition to facilities. The seaway could not be defended against air attack or sabotage, the Chicago organization asserted, and defending it could cause a manpower drain. In fact, the use of manpower and material to build it would actually be detrimental to our national defense efforts.

In terms of the transportation issues, the Chicago group said the Seaway was not needed . . . that it would not be self liquidating . . . that present transportation facilities were adequate . . . that Corps of Engineers estimates were wrong and, including harbor improvements, the Seaway would cost nearly $2.5

President Eisenhower is presented a bronze medallion replica of the seal of the St. Lawrence Seaway Development Corporation, on the second anniversary of his signing the Wiley-Dondero Seaway Act, May 13, 1954. The President is shown with Senator Alexander Wiley of Wisconsin and other Seaway officials. In background is a drawing of the Seaway's Eisenhower Lock (formerly known as Robinson Bay Lock).

The Great Lakes-to-Tidewater St. Lawrence River ship canal project is not a dead issue. In fact, it has become a live factor on the present presidential campaign, and it is indicated that it will be much in the forefront in the next Congress. Senator Brookhart of Iowa says that the St. Lawrence waterway project ought to be completed through the joint action of the United States and Canada in the shortest possible time. And he sees no reason why the question of the proposed all-American canal through New York state should stand in the way of the St. Lawrence waterway. It may be feasible to develop both outlets from the lakes to the sea.

From "Michigan Farmer" September 29, 1928

billion rather than the $982 million estimated by the Corps. They said that a 27-foot draft was not sufficient, and that a 35-foot draft would be needed—and that this would cost more than $4 billion.

And there was more. A lot more.

Thomas A. Murray, New York State Chairman of the American Federation of Labor cried, "The harmful effect of the proposed Seaway on labor is beyond calculation.The workers engaged in transportation, storage, handling, trucking of cargo, ship repair, ship supplies and those who work in waterfront refineries, assembly plants and other industries located in New York harbor, when summed up total hundreds of thousands, and for every direct worker in these basic trades, there are others in local retailing and service trades . . ."

Rear Admiral F. R. Harris, USN, Ret., remarked that "The St. Lawrence Seaway . . . would add nothing to our national defense; on the contrary, it would burden us with additional responsibility."

The final guns had been fired.

It was now time—and for certain, the last time—for a vote on U.S. participation in the St. Lawrence Seaway.

Everything that was to be said had been said.

That same month, on the other side of the Hill, the Senate Foreign Relations Committee approved the Wiley bill 13 to 2, but Congress adjourned before further action could be taken.

Early in 1954, the Administration went to work again in earnest for the Wiley bill—and through a series of political maneuvers, succeeding in finding the votes to pass it 51 to 53. On May 6, 1954 the House, by a vote of 241-158 passed the Dondero bill, and with the Senate's acceptance of a few minor changes in the House bill, the Wiley-Dondero Seaway Act was passed.

And so, after defeats in 1918, 1934, 1942, 1944, 1948 and 1952, after Canadian delays in 1914, 1922 and procrastination in the whole decades of 1920-30, a joint U.S.-Canadian Seaway was, at least and at last on paper, a reality.

The fight had been won.

3

Construction of the Seaway

There was a kind of jubiliation all along the St. Lawrence Valley when the news broke that the United States has voted to join Canada in the Seaway project, and that construction of the waterway was soon to begin.

Jubilation: Perhaps that was the official word for it.

Relief might have said it better.

For long years the region had suffered the artificial, superimposed depressed economy of a region defined by uncertainty or, even worse, awaiting possible annihilation. Why paint your house? It might be torn down next year. Why expand a business, or open a new one? Both business and customers might be in the way of progress—a sure prerequisite to destruction.

For as many years as most people wished to remember, the St. Lawrence Valley, or huge parts of it, had simply marked time, or as some would wryly put it, had tread water, waiting for the Seaway to be built. But now at long last, the uncertainty was over: For good or for bad . . . the period of stagnation was at an end.

Slowly, realization came to many homeowners—over 8,000 in Ontario, over a thousand in New York (not to mention the more than a thousand owners of summer homes along the picturesque reaches of the St. Lawrence)—that their homes were to be destroyed. They were being ordered to move. It was the Ontario Hydro, on the Canadian side and the New York Power people on the U.S. side who were giving the orders. And there really wasn't a great deal anybody could do about it.

Worse, or just as bad, was the fact that the power companies were paying market value (plus a small percentage bonus for inconvenience) for the homes they were condemning, rather than paying replacement value of the homes. And, of course, the market values had been badly depressed in the first place by the everpresent shadow of the Seaway.

In Canada, primarily seven communities and part of an eighth were affected; the villages of Iroquois and Morrisburg (all of Iroquois was to be razed and better than half of Morrisburg)

Giant cranes on railroad tracks assist early lock construction.

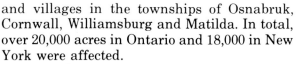

First blast which began construction of the St. Lawrence Seaway took place place near Montreal on November 17, 1954.

Crews stand by during blasting near St. Lambert, first lock in the Seaway System.

and villages in the townships of Osnabruk, Cornwall, Williamsburg and Matilda. In total, over 20,000 acres in Ontario and 18,000 in New York were affected.

Ontario home owners, upset over the proposed payments of Ontario Hydro, took their complaints of unfair reimbursement to their local governments, which in turn raised a clamor which was heard all the way to the Canadian capitol at Ottawa. As a result, a St. Lawrence Board of Review was established to which homeowners could appeal what they felt were the unfair prices offered by Hydro.

Southwest of the old 14-ft. Lachine Canal, at the infamous Lachine Rapids, was a Mohawk Indian reservation which had been deeded to the Mohawk nation in perpetuity. Called the Caughnawaga, it was directly in the way of Seaway progress: Some 1300 acres were needed for flooding to conquer the rapids.

Looking west along center line of Long Sault Canal, U.S. Section of the St. Lawrence Seaway Project. Grasse River Lock construction is seen in the center of the photo. The soil in foreground is famous Marine Clay which created immense delays and cost increases in Seaway construction.

Of course the Indians protested the acquisition of their land, citing their treaty. But their protests fell upon deaf ears—the treaty was "cancelled." Their case became one of many, many well publicized court suits, appeals, complaints and other forms of outcry which met the men who forged the route of the Seaway by lawbook and condemnation.

Legal complaints notwithstanding, it may be said in retrospect that despite the clamor and chaos, most homeowners (and the Indians) received fair and satisfactory reimbursement for their property.

One of the ways of achieving this satisfaction for homeowners came in the form of three new communities which Ontario Hydro planned to produce. Entirely new towns complete with schools, churches, shopping areas, all designed carefully to fit the needs—supposedly—of the ousted villages. The town of New Iroquois, just a mile from its namesake, was to care for that population. The town which was eventually called Long Sault was to take in the Moulinette and Mille Roches populations, and Ingleside was to care for Aultsville, Farrans Point, Dickinsons Landing and Wales. A new business section would be added to Morrisburg to replace the more than half of the town that would be soon under water.

Photo above shows home being moved away from area to be flooded during construction of the Seaway project.

The new town of Long Sault: aerial view at right, street scene at left.

But the planners in Montreal and Toronto and Ottawa had not really considered the economics of the matter, and it soon became evident that, nice though they might be, the new towns were beyond the economic reach of large groups of ousted homeowners. The prices they were receiving for their homes—*market value* prices (plus the 10-15% inconvenience bonus) was not enough to let them afford to build new homes at *current-valued* prices. As well, many of the people being evicted were elderly, and did not want to be involved, or could not afford to be involved, in a new mortgage.

The solution to this problem made newspaper headlines all over the world. Hydro, contracting with a U.S. firm for the use of gigantic movers, now offered to move any house that was in the way of the Seaway to a brand new site—to put that house on a new foundation, complete with a basement, paint and landscape the house—all for free.

And so here was a good, viable alternative for the homeowners: they could sell or they could keep their houses and have them moved and vastly improved. The housemovers, gargantuan pieces of equipment, were capable of moving houses so gently that the owners had

Unique housemoving equipment was so sensitive that housewives could leave dishes in the cupboard, furniture where it stood.

Engineering photo shows Eisenhower Lock under construction in September, 1956. Note concrete plant at lower left.

Guide wall and substantial elevation of lock walls can be seen in photo of same lock, taken nine months later, in May, 1957.

View shows landlocked lock under construction near Long Sault Canal. St. Lawrence River is seen at bottom, while Grasse River runs along left side of photo. Aerial was made in September, 1956.

Highway tunnel entries can be seen at top of photo in this June, 1958, photo of nearly completed Eisenhower lock.

no need to even remove their furniture or tie down their belongings. Most houses were moved intact.

The world press loved that story, and Hydro appeared to be something of a folk hero after the episode.

Regarding plans for the new towns, many of the new residents felt that they simply would not do. So a board was formed, consisting of the Ontario Provincial Department of Planning and Development, Ontario Hydro, and the municipal governments of old towns. All had to agree on plans for each new town before it could be actually constructed. By 1958 they were virtually completed.

On both sides of the river, churches were moved, whole cemeteries (18 in Ontario alone), highways, railways, sewage systems, schools, utility systems, factories, farms, businesses— entire sociological and cultural entities—were transplanted.

Soon, the still waters of the new Seaway would forever hide every trace of the lives and the histories of those towns, their people and their times.

Of course, while the difficult and thankless activity of moving the people was underway, construction had begun on the Seaway itself.

The New York Times said it best perhaps, calling the building of the St. Lawrence project "in the fullest sense, a battle with the river.

"No job could . . . be completed, no slides cut through, no dam poured—without considering the temperament of the water's flow," the *Times* said.

The job, the total job, staggered the imagination. Not just the building of the world's second largest hydroelectric dam, this. It meant building canals and dikes and dams and immense locks and bridges. It meant making tunnels, relocating highways and railways, moving and resettling entire communities, as we have already seen. It was an incredible, vast job of moving and bringing under control one of the largest rivers on the North American continent.

Photo shows Moses-Saunders Power Dam under construction.

The construction consortium established to build the Seaway consisted of the U.S. Army Corps of Engineers, hired by the St. Lawrence Seaway Development Corporation (SLSDC), and Hall and Rich, an affiliate of Boston's Charles T. Main Engineers, hired by the New York Power Authority. The St. Lawrence Seaway Authority, SLSDC's Canadian counterpart, called upon engineers from its own government's Department of Transport, and Ontario Hydro brought in its own people.

Specialists from all over the world soon became a part of the project, testing everything from soil to water to concrete to steel, and like an army of worker ants, sometimes greatly organized, more often working with *a priori* judgments, the construction companies, their experts, consultants, advisers, technicians, specialists, skilled and unskilled laborers, their monstrous equipment rumbling like Paleolithic behemouths, their rock splitting dynamite,

field offices and yes, their red tape—set themselves to the task of taking fresh water to meet salt water.

In the International Section, the gigantic Moses-Saunders Power Dam was to be built across the northern channel of the St. Lawrence between Barnhart Island and the Ontario mainland. Two smaller dams—the Iroquois and Long Sault—were to be built farther upstream, the former across the south channel of the river near Iroquois, Ontario and the latter stretching from Barnhart Island.

The job that faced the construction combine was to literally dry up the St. Lawrence River and send it somewhere else so that these three dams could be built. Cofferdams were built to dry up half of the river at a time for the construction of the two smaller dams. When, for each, half a dam was completed, the flow of the river was diverted through the gates of the completed portions, the cofferdams destroyed, and the remaining part of the dam built in the newly dried out area.

A huge cofferdam also diverted the flow of the St. Lawrence from the north to the south channel around Barnhart Island to allow work to begin on the giant $600 million Moses Saunders Power Dam.

A temporary pontoon bridge was built between the U.S. and Barnhart Island, at a cost in excess of a million dollars, to allow American construction teams to reach the power dam site. Under the construction agreement, the United States and Canada were each to build their halves of the jointly owned dam, meeting in the middle when the project was done.

Over 1,000 construction contracts were let by both governments for the Seaway project, in-cluding many to European firms. The Perini Corporation of Framingham, Massachusetts, headed up a joint venture of contracting firms which included Boise's Morrison-Knudsen Co.; Omaha's Peter Kiewet Sons' Co.; Walsh Construction of New York City, and the Utah Construction Co. of San Francisco.

The entire world was talking about the immense engineering feat—the greatest in history, most agreed—of building the 360-mile waterway. It was by every definition the world's third great man-made waterway, excelling in scope the 100-mile Suez, built at a cost of $84 million in 1914 or the 50-mile Panama Canal, built in 1869 at a cost of $402 million.

Excavation of the Seaway became a nightmare of gigantic proportion. The earth threw everything it had at the construction teams,

Later construction photo of Moses-Saunders Power Dam.

The power dam as it appears today. Note Long Sault Dam in upper left of photo.

Photo shows flooded channel in July, 1958.

Looking west along South Cornwall Channel, downstrean of Snell Lock, with Cornwall Island shown at right. One span of Roosevelt Bridge and approach spans of the High Level Bridge can be seen in center.

Steel stop-logs are shown being placed in the closure structure of a dike which impounds the waters of Lake St. Lawrence before flooding of the new lake. The closure is at the upstream end of the Cornwall Canal.

Excavation and dredging meet in this 1958 photo of an 18 mile canal excavated overland and behind cofferdams. The canal begins in the Montreal Harbor and follows the south shore of the St. Lawrence River where it meets the 27 ft. deep channel dredged in Lake St. Louis.

Construction of Cote. Ste. Catherine, second Canadian lock in the system.

The beginning of the approach wall at lower Beauharnois, with concrete cribs built on land then transported to their numbered position where they are weighted and sunk. Note dredge in background.

The start, in September 1954, of the Long Sault Cofferdam between the American shore and Long Sault Island.

Installation of lock gates at Massena, New York, site of two U.S. Seaway locks.

Placement of giant lock gates at Cote. Ste. Catherine.

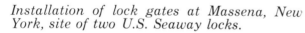

Nearly a mile of completed channel curves by the Lachine Rapids, near Montreal.

Lock construction begins at St. Lambert in July, 1952.

A wall of solid limestone 40 feet high towers above excavation equipment at Lachine Section.

Equipment at work, digging and hauling.

Long Sault Dam as it appears today.

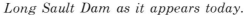

Aerial view of Jacques Cartier Bridge under construction in 1955.

Construction close-up at Jacques Cartier Bridge below shows the "translation operation" at the bridge—the spectacular and complicated replacement of a 248-foot deck truss span with a through truss structure to provide ship clearance. The job was accomplished by Dominion Bridge Company engineers and erection workers on a Sunday morning. The project involved moving the old span out along runways on the downstream side, while the new span, complete in all details including a surfaced asphalt roadway and sidewalk, was inched into position from runways upstream. Both spans were linked together and a total of 3100 tons of steel was shifted a distance of 78 feet in a little under five hours. The operation was part of the general bridge raising project on the southern section of the Montreal bridge.

Looking downstream toward the lower guide wall of Eisenhower lock.

from shale at the two Lachine locks to tough sandstone which had to be drilled and blasted at Upper and Lower Beauharnois.

At Eisenhower Lock in the International Section, a heavy glacial till that "weighed like concrete" when wet and, when dry, was "hard as concrete," drove the giant equipment off the job in total defeat. At Snell Lock, what was known as marine clay presented a similar obstacle. Firm in the ground, it became soft when excavated and was impossible to dump— it stuck like glue to the truck beds.

Everywhere, it seemed, the earth was rebelling. A number of firms defaulted on their excavation contracts or went bankrupt trying to fulfill them. Eventually new contracts had to be written, old ones modified and contract figures raised—some doubled—to permit the painful, yard-by-yard excavation to continue.

Excavation contractors claimed over $100 million in extra payments, allowing that they had not been given accurate or complete soil specifications on which to bid. For a while, tempers got a bit short. Even the once-harmonious lead agencies fell to bickering. Prodded on by Robert W. Moses, whose ill temper was as widely known as his reputation for building parks, arguments arose over a multiplicity of issues. One such argument was the question of who would dredge the south channel of the St. Lawrence, below the power dam. SLSDC said it was power's responsibility. Moses, in turn, accused SLSDC, then, of course, under the direction of Lewis Castle, of trying to beg off the job in order to save money for the navigation interests. He attacked the Corps for bad cost estimates. (The Corps had estimated the original U.S. Seaway costs at about $88 million, but by 1956 costs were already approaching the $105 debt limit fixed by Congress, and the Seaway was not nearly completed.) After a great deal of argument, a decision was reached whereby the two power entities would contribute $6 million each for the dredging project and the two navigation entities, the balance, approximately $20 million more.

Administrator Castle planned to go back to Congress to ask that the Seaway debt limit be raised to $122 million, but by the time he was ready to make his request, costs had risen to the point that he felt a $140 million limit was needed. Canada, too, had money problems. The Seaway Authority asked Parliament for an increase from a $300 to a $355 million debt limit.

Castle and Chevrier went to battle with the irritable Moses again over the issue of a low span of the Roosevelt Highway and Rail Bridge—a bridge which was to be removed to permit ship passage. The original plan was to relocate the bridge and tie it into a park which Moses was planning. New highway and rail connections, plus three smaller bridges would have to be constructed as part of the effort to move the bridge. The navigation interests felt they could talk the New York Central Railroad into abandoning its route to Corwall and Ottawa (it did not pay well for them) and, in turn, they could then build a less expensive, more attractive, higher highway bridge at the same site.

Moses raged. He hurled accusations and insults at Castle. But in the end, the navigation interests won out and the graceful International Bridge was built between the U.S. and Canada at Saunders Island.

Construction continued, despite the continuing heat of battles such as these. There were seven new locks to be built—five by Canada, two by the Americans. Over 22,000 men were to dig up 210,000,000 cubic yards of earth and rock: Piled upon a football field, it would create a uniformly distributed mountain 22½ miles high. There were 6,000,000 cubic yards of concrete to be poured, enough for a four-lane highway reaching from London to Rome.

The Americans dug nearly a million cubic yards of earth to make the 800-ft. Snell and Eisenhower locks. Seven dredges, thirty-two scows and barges worked in the International Rapids section alone. Assigned to that section were 136 steam shovels, 311 tractors and 429 pieces of railroad rolling stock.

Each minute step in the construction process found new problems, took new creative solutions to master them. Take concreting: How did you get concrete from mixer to dam or lock? Mixers poured the wet cement not into truck beds, but into two "buckets" that travelled in the beds. A gantry crane picked up the buckets, dumping them into wooden forms where the wet concrete had the air worked out of it and was solidified into blocks.

Work continued, day and night, month in, month out, year by year. Through the biting cold of the St. Lawrence Valley—where temperatures often plummet to 50 below—the pouring, the ironwork, the electrical and carpentry went on. Relentlessly, around the clock, pin-point figures of men could be seen up and down cliff-like walls of the mighty power dam, across its top, in an unbelievable cacophony of motion and noise and light. The sight was awe inspiring.

Americans and Canadians, on identical halves of the power dam, used different construction techniques, different kinds of equipment, different solutions to common problems, and often, different languages, but miracles of miracles—the two halves met, the dam construction was complete.

This photo was taken June 26, 1959, during the ceremonies marking the official opening of the St. Lawrence Seaway by her Majesty, Queen Elizabeth II, and President Eisenhower, and shows the royal party on the official platform acknowledging the playing of the national anthems. The ceremonies were held in an area located a short distance downstream of the St. Lambert lock, across the river from Montreal.

Over-all physical construction of the Seaway from Montreal to the Welland was divided into five sections. At the Lachine Section, from Montreal 31 miles up-river, a Canadian project involved the building of ten new bridges, alteration of several more, channel dredging and construction of the first two locks of the Seaway—the St. Lambert and Cote Ste. Catherine. The La Prairie Basin Canal, 18 miles long and extending from Montreal to Lake St. Louis was also dug by the Canadians in this section.

The Soulanges section, sixteen miles further along, was also Canadian, with construction including the two-mile Beauharnois canal and the Upper and Lower Beauharnois Locks.

The Lake St. Francis section of the Seaway stretched 29 miles. Here Canada's biggest effort was dredging.

The International Rapids section, next, some 44 miles from Cornwall to Chimney Point, was the greatest challenge for the makers of the Seaway. Here, of course, the two American locks—Eisenhower and Snell—were built, the

Great Lakes passenger cruise ships pass through the Eisenhower Lock at Massena, N.Y., on June 26, 1959, enroute to Montreal to witness Queen Elizabeth and President Eisenhower officially open the Seaway the following day. The ships returned to Massena on June 27 when Vice President Nixon welcomed the Queen at Eisenhower Lock. The aerial view shows the pioneer passenger cruise ships, SS South American (right) and SS North American. The Cleveland Press and the Cleveland Chamber of Commerce chartered the South American while the Chicago Association of Commerce and Industry chartered her sister ship for the "Meet The Queen Cruise." The ships were landmarks on the Great Lakes for 40 years, and were operated by Chicago, Duluth and Georgian Bay Transit Company, of Chicago.

Dignitaries gather to chat informally at the Seaway locks at Massena. Shown in this historic photo are Great Britain's Queen Elizabeth II and her husband the Duke of Edinburgh, while at left a youthful Vice President and Mrs. Richard Nixon look on.

President Dwight D. Eisenhower and Queen Elizabeth II are escorted on a tour of facilities during Seaway Dedication in June, 1959.

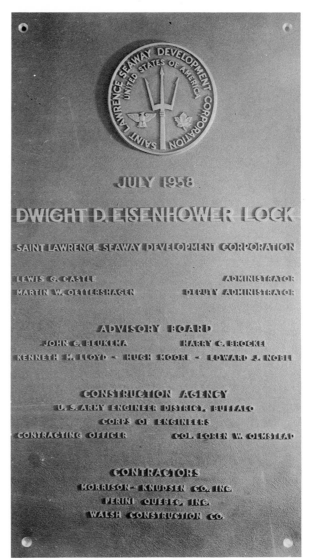

Plaque at Eisenhower Lock.

Secretary of the Army Wilbur M. Brucker made the principal addresses during ceremonies marking the opening of the Dwight D. Eisenhower and Bertrand H. Snell Locks of the St. Lawrence Seaway. The Secretary of the Army supervised St. Lawrence Seaway construction as a representative of the President and Secretary of Defense. Secretary Brucker is shown greeting Foster Winter, member of the Board of Directors, Great Lakes St. Lawrence Seaway Association. Others are L to R: Assistant Secretary of the Army George H. Roderick, Grand Rapids, Michigan, Congressman George A. Dondero, after whom the Wiley-Dondero Canal of the St. Lawrence Seaway was named; Secretary Brucker, Mr. Winter and Secretary of the Treasury Robert B. Anderson.

Vice President Richard M. Nixon and Prince Philip chat informally at lectern.

At Seaway Opening Ceremonies, Mrs. Richard M. Nixon; Vice President Nixon; Senator Kenneth Keating; Governor Rockefeller's daughter; Governor Nelson A. Rockefeller, Mrs. Javits and Senator Jacob Javits.

Canadian Iroquois lock, the mile-long Iroquois Canal, the Moses Saunders Power Dam, the Long Sault and Cornwall dams and, of course, the cofferdams and the 10-mile long Wiley-Dondero ship Canal which bypasses the dams.

The Thousand Island section, sixty-eight miles in length, needed only channel improvement and the removing of rock shoals.

By Spring, 1958, it appeared that most of the work on the Seaway would be completed on schedule. Unobserved, really, during the construction, yet emerging to public notice as the project neared completion was the incredible cooperation that had existed between Americans and Canadians. Working side by side, ignoring all national origins and boundaries, men from two different nations had worked together, hand in hand, on a common project.

And really, no one had thought much about it at the time.

But it became apparent to the people of both the United States and Canada that without that international cooperation—not between governments, but between men, sick-tired covered with marine clay and concrete dust,

Dignitaries disembarking from plane at Massena, N.Y., on June 3, 1956 for dedication ceremony.

Seaway Administrator Lewis G. Castle speaks at dedication of Eisenhower Lock.

men bruised and cursing and cold—the project could not have been completed on time, if indeed at all.

Now that it was virtually finished, what of the costs? The two power agencies had remained within budget spending $300 million each, but the Canadian Seaway entitity was over 80 percent over the budget at $322 million and the U.S. 42 percent over at $124 million.

On July 1, 1958, the gates of the Moses Saunders and Long Sault Dams were closed. The rock cofferdam that had been built across the north channel of the St. Lawrence was blown up and 38,000 acres of land disappeared under water. Soon ships would sail straightway into the lakes.

It was soon time to put away the tools, and celebrate.

The Seaway opened on April 25, 1959 and was dedicated on June 26 by President Eisenhower and Queen Elizabeth II at St. Lambert Lock, where the royal yacht, Britannia, crossed through ceremonial gates at the approach to the lock, to mark the official opening of the Seaway.

Looking aft from the bridge of the Cliffs Victory.

Above and below, typical Seaway "Salties".

Constricted channels in the Seaway system are busy water highways between the lakes.

Tight fit in U.S. Seaway lock

Commemorative stamps of similar design were issued by the U.S. and Canadian Post Offices to celebrate the opening of the St. Lawrence Seaway.

Except for the necessary differences in captions and denominations, the stamps were identical—the result of the cooperative efforts of Canadian artists A. L. Pollock and Gerald Trottier, and American artists William H. Buckley, Arnold J. Copeland and Ervine Metzl.

The stamps were both first class denomination: five cents for Canada and four cents for the United States. Forty million of the Canadian stamps and 120 million of the American stamps were issued.

The Canadian stamp was bilingual with the heading "St. Lawrence Seaway" and "Voie Maritime Du St-Laurent," and the caption "Postage" and "Postes" reproduced in both English and French. The United States version carries the caption "St. Lawrence Seaway" across the top of the stamp, "United States" across the bottom; and the wording "Postage" at the left and the denomination at the right.

The stamps for both nations were printed in red and blue on white paper thereby utilizing the national colors of both countries.

Reproduced in white on both stamps were the emblems of both nations, the Maple Leaf for Canada, and the Eagle for the United States, enclosed in inter-locking links superimposed over a background of the Great Lakes.

The Canadian stamp had its "First Day of Issue" cancellation in Ottawa, while the first-day sale of the American stamp was at Massena, New York, the site of the St. Lawrence Seaway Development Corporation in the United States. The pictorial cancellation used on first-day covers at Massena featured the Seal of the Seaway Development Corporation.

The two stamps were placed on sale on June 26, 1959, the date on which the opening ceremony was held by both countries.

Postmaster General Arthur E. Summerfield in announcing the release of the stamp in Washington said:

"The joint issuance of these stamps by Canada and the United States is one more instance of the increasingly close relationship between our two nations. The St. Lawrence Seaway is a monument to the efforts of two sovereign nations and an outstanding example of international cooperation and good will."

Postmaster General William Hamilton in Ottawa responded in a similar vein:

"The St. Lawrence Seaway is an outstanding example of what has been achieved through the friendly cooperation of Canada and the United States, each dedicated to peaceful advancement of all mankind. At a time when international trade is so vital to the people of the free world, our joint stamp issue salutes the opening of a new link in a vastly improved channel for such trade and a powerful source of hydro-electric energy for both our nations."

It was the first occasion that Canada and the United States have ever issued a stamp jointly.

A busy day at the Welland.

4

The Seaway System

The first year of Seaway operation saw 20.6 million tons of cargo transit the Montreal-Lake Ontario section. There was a great sense of adventure along the new inland sea (some called it the Mediterranean of North America), as its ports battled with state and city governments for money to expand their facilities.

They advertised grandly. Duluth (Minn.) and Superior (Wisc.), two ports so close together that they shared a common harbor, called themselves one, with the slogan, "The world's greatest inland port."

Duluth-Superior already boasted 13 grain elevators with a 55 million bushel capacity, another million-bushel elevator was being built and more were being contemplated; a new three-vessel terminal with two giant gantry cranes was also under construction. The twin ports advertised themselves as providing the doorway to "a vast area rich in exportable commodities and eager to process and consume goods from the eastern United States and foreign lands."

Rochester, (N.Y.), on the southern seaboard of Lake Erie, advertised industrial sites and noted that the Seaway has made the city an "important port of entry for national and international marine traffic." Nearby Oswego (N.Y.) said just about the same thing—adding however, that it was spending $2.5 million for an outer breakwall.

The small port of Kenosha (Wisc.) called itself the gateway to the world, and redrew the map to show that the Wisconsin port was indeed the true hub of the nation.

A $20 million reclamation program was announced by Hamilton (Ont.) which included a new $4 million lift bridge and a substantial dredging program to let larger ships into the harbor. Milwaukee (Wisc.) worked both sides of the street, talking both about the new Seaway and about the business it was picking up from the Illinois and Mississippi River Waterway System.

Everybody was talking industrial sites.

Even Cleveland, home of the lake carriers and one of the major rail hubs of the midwest, once an arch foe of the Seaway, was selling land which was touted to be tied into "that unmatched transportation network—the St. Lawrence Seaway." The Seaway Center, as Cleveland called itself, was still another gateway to the world.

As the ports vied for the attention of the shippers, the Seaway was becoming an entirely new and different experience for the men who guided the big ships to their destinations.

What was it like to travel this inland water route? One sea captain said, "There is no waterway like it in the whole world. It's no easy traffic, but the grandeur of the river, the roaring of Niagara Falls, the endless chain of lakes and islands makes it highly attractive. It can be ranked among the best in the world in technical and navigational equipment and in traffic organization and control."

Lockage at Beauharnois.

Cote Ste. Catherine, the second Seaway lock.

The five Great Lakes, contrary to what most people think, are not really contiguous. They do not connect to each other; rather, they are joined by a series of connecting channels—by rivers. The St. Marys River section of the Seaway system joins Lake Superior with the four lower lakes and creates the northernmost Michigan boundary separating that state and Ontario. Here, the second great lockage system of the Great Lakes is located: Sault St. Marie.

The famous Sault (pronounced, and often spelled, "Soo") had been a navigation bottleneck for the Great Lakes since the earliest days of water transportation. A nineteen-foot fall in the St. Marys River, slight though it was, had become a barrier which ground inter-lake navigation to a complete halt. Ships downbound from Superior and upbound from the other four lakes were forced to unload their cargoes at the Sault. The cargoes were then carried overland for a full mile until they could be loaded aboard another ship, nineteen feet higher in the water, from which their journey would continue.

In 1850, two Michigan senators, Alpheus Felch and Lewis Cass convinced Congress that for the good of the region a canal was needed at the Sault.

The Fairbanks Scale Company and the State of Michigan signed a construction contract (in 1853) and within two years a lock and canal had been completed at the Sault, ending the mile-long overland portage. The Canal was 5500 feet long—just over a mile—115 feet wide and 12 feet deep, with stone walls 25 feet high and 10 feet thick. The Canal housed two locks, each 350 feet high and 70 feet wide. The upper lock raised or lowered ships eight feet, the lower lock, ten feet.

The cost: just $200 short of a million dollars.

Congress had given Michigan 750,000 acres of public land with which to pay for the canal—and it was this land which the builders, now known as the St. Marys Falls Ship Canal Company, took in payment, including nearly 40,000 acres in the northern iron ranges, 147,000 acres in the Michigan copper country and another 560,000 acres of timberland. Based upon the cost of the canal, the land went to the builder at a value of something like $1.20 per acre.

Around 1870, Michigan's state geologist, Alexander Winchell, proposed the construction of a canal between Au Train and Little Bay de Noc, near Green Bay connecting Lakes Superior and Michigan and eliminating the need for the 300 to 350 haul through the Soo. The proposed Canal, about 40 miles in length, followed existing waterways.

Although it was studied for several years, and made some newspaper headlines, the proposed canal never really got off the ground.

Between 1876 and 1896 two new larger locks—the Weitzel and the Poe—replaced the original Michigan State locks at the Soo. The Weitzel was 515 feet long and 80 feet wide, while the Poe was 800 feet long and 100 feet wide, making it, at the time, the largest lock in the world.

Ford machine parts on the Seaway.

Historic photo shows "old State Locks" at Sault Ste. Marie, 1856.

Returning Area Engineer Clifford A. Aune (left) is presented with a special commendation by Col. Leonard J. Goodsell, Executive Director of the Great Lakes Commission, on behalf of the eight Great Lakes states. Aune had been in charge of the "Soo" since 1929.

The locks at Sault Ste. Marie—the famous "Soo"—today.

Ore carrier emerges from Sault Ste. Marie lock, while another enters lock on other side of Corps of Engineers building.

The two locks this time were built not by a private contractor but rather by the U.S. Army Corps of Engineers, who also ran the Soo (and still do) and who have named all the locks since then after generals. Weitzel Lock was named for General Godfrey Weitzel, who directed work on the lock and the Poe Lock was named for General Orlando M. Poe, Weitzel's successor as Army Engineer. Interestingly, the engineer who designed the Weitzel Lock, a civilian named Alfred Noble, later became one of the leading figures in the construction of the Panama Canal.

To the north of the U.S. canals, Canada later constructed a 900-foot lock which was somewhat deeper than the Poe. Larger ships used this canal until 1914 when the 1350-foot Davis Lock was built. Longer than the Panama Canal locks by 350 feet, the Davis lock was twinned before it was completed. The twin lock—the fourth for the Soo—was called the Sabin.

The four locks functioned efficiently for more than three decades, until World War II, when the smallest, the Weitzel, was replaced with a lock that matched the specifications of the

Poe—800 feet long and 80 feet wide. It was named after General Douglas MacArthur.

Construction began on the new lock in 1963: 1,200 feet long, 110 feet wide and 32 feet draft. Completed in 1969 (just in time to help celebrate the 10th Anniversary of the Seaway) it was named for the lock it replaced, the Poe.

The Soo, by 1950, was reputed to be moving more cargo through its locks than the combined tonnage of the Panama, Suez, Kiel and Manchester canals combined.

Today a staff of some 300 people run the "Soo" Locks for the Corps of Engineers. In 1974-75, the Soo operated for 12 uninterrupted months, the first time for such a feat, to record well over a hundred million tons of transiting cargo. (See Chapter VIII.)

Aerial view of U.S. Sault Ste. Marie locks: Davis, Sabin, Poe and MacArthur

In 1975 the Corps initiated a study to determine the economic value of replacing the Sabin Lock with another lock the size of the Poe, or larger. The apparent need for a second large lock has arisen out of the growing use of larger and wider lake ships—the 1,000 foot landlocked behemoths that carry iron pellets along the water route from Superior to the south.

The question has been frequently asked why the St. Lawrence Seaway Development Corporation, operators of the Seaway locks on the St. Lawrence River, and the U.S. agency primarily responsible for cargo activity in the System, does not operate the locks at the Soo. The only good reason to emerge is that, apparently, the Corps was there first.

Moving toward the sea, the next connecting channel in the Great Lakes-St. Lawrence Seaway system is the Detroit River Section. Here no locks are needed—the only lock-free connecting channel in the system. This channel ties Lakes Erie and Ontario with Huron, Michigan and Superior. Every ship— ocean or lake carrier—that travels from the three upper lakes must transit the Detroit River, one of the busiest of rivers in the world.

Downbound, the third river section in the lakes is the Welland which houses the world famous stairstep Welland Canal locks.

The 27½ mile Welland Canal was first opened to commercial traffic in 1829. Built to allow ships to travel around the great Niagara Es-

Ore boats move along Detroit River—one of world's busiest—under Ambassador Bridge.

Ship passes through Welland Canal.

Another aerial view of Welland locks four, five and six, twinned and in flight. Together they lift or lower ships 140 feet.

Aerial view shows part of Welland lock system.

carpment between Lakes Erie and Ontario, the Canal runs from Port Colborne in Lake Erie to Port Robinson, on the Chippawa River, which empties into Lake Ontario, a drop of 326 feet from lake to lake.

At that time, 40 locks were necessary to raise or lower ships between the lakes.

A second construction phase began in 1873 when the locks were enlarged to 270x45 feet, with a 14 feet draft. The 40 locks were reduced to 25 in number.

A third reconstruction began in 1913, and the locks became virtually as we know them today: Each lock has a 46 ft. lift, is 80 feet wide and has a draft of 30 feet.

Considerable improvements to the Canal were made in the 1950's in order to bring it up to Seaway standards. Locks one through seven are lift locks; the eighth is a guard lock. The three flight locks, (officially known as four, five and six) are twinned—that is, there are two of each, to handle traffic coming and going simultaneously between Erie and Ontario.

A channel relocation project, completed after six years in 1974 at a cost of $188 million, took many of the kinks and bends out of the original Canal. Previously, ships were required to navigate a 192-foot section of the canal through the City of Welland, with six bridges and many narrow bends. The new 83 mile bypass (see map) is 350 feet wide and was created east of the city.

Tonnages through the canal have grown from 27½ million tons in 1959 to more than 62 million tons in 1970.

The final connecting channel, of course, is the lakes-to-the-Sea section, the St. Lawrence River. From Lake Ontario to the Seaway Locks, the St. Lawrence is one of the most picturesque and idyllic sections of any river on the North American continent. Called Thousand Islands, or Manitoanna ("Garden Place of the Great Spirit," by the Indians) the region was once the playground of millionnaires, who built stately homes—palaces, really—on the thousand or more islands that dot the river. Sightseers regularly travel upstate New York highways to

the seven-mile long Thousand Island Bridge, from which over 200 of these islands can be seen. More than a million cars cross the bridge each year, taking in the view, which is said to be duplicated in grandeur and beauty only on the lower reaches of the Rhine.

The picturesque Thousand Island section runs between the Tibbets Point Lighthouse at Cape Vincent to the end of the island chain near the City of Ogdensburg. Here, the St. Lawrence becomes commercial again, and the mighty locks of the Seaway become the dominant attractions.

All seven Seaway locks are 766 feet in length from breast well to gate feeder, meaning that ships entering the locks must be no longer than 730 feet. Each lock is 80 feet wide, with a depth over stills of 30 feet.

Proceeding eastward, or downbound, from the lakes to the sea, the first of the St. Lawrence Locks is the Iroquois, which lowers ships from 5 to 6 feet downstream. Nearby Eisenhower Lock lowers ships from 38 to 42 feet and its companion, Snell Lock, 45 to 49 feet. The Beauharnois, next in the chain, lowers ships 36 to 40 and 38 to 42 feet respectively for the upper and lower lock. Cote Ste. Catherine drops the ships another 33 to 35 feet, and the last lock out to the sea, St. Lambert, drops them a final 13 to 20 feet to tidewater.

The three Seaway dams deserve specific mention, although they are not tied directly into Seaway navigation.

The smallest of the three, the Iroquois Control Dam, is located 25 miles upstream from the Moses-Saunders Power Dam. It regulates the outflow from the watershed of the Great Lakes into Lake St. Lawrence, the pool whose waters are used for power.

Extending from the U.S. mainland to Canada, the dam consists of 32 openings which are controlled by lift gates. The gates are operated by two 320-ton gantry cranes. The dam was built at a cost of $14.4 million.

The Long Sault Control Dam is just 3½ miles above the Moses Saunders Power Dam. It controls the water flow into the South channel

The Welland By-Pass Channel.

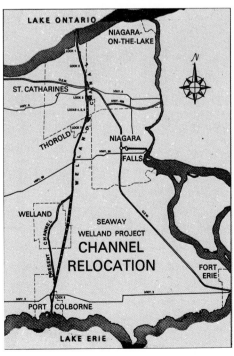

Map shows Welland By-Pass Channel.

Locks operate 24 hours a day.

Thousand Island section of St. Lawrence River, dotted with expensive homes, even castles, make the river an American reproduction of the Rhine.

An early view of St. Lambert Lock at Montreal.

of the St. Lawrence River. It also controls the depth of the power pool.

Entirely in the U.S., the dam was built at a cost of $25.7 million. Thirty 50-foot lift gates are operated by 18 fixed, 175-ton hoists and by traveling cranes.

The gigantic $36 million Moses Saunders Power Dam, owned jointly by the U.S. and Canada, produces 13 billion kilowatt hours of energy output annually. Thirty-two turbines and generators are located in the Power dam—

sixteen in each half. Water to produce the power is provided by the 28-mile long Lake St. Lawrence, an artificial lake and power pool which was created by the Seaway project.

The Robert H. Saunders-St. Lawrence generating system in Canada and the Robert Moses Power Dam in the U.S. are adjoining powerhouses which, along with the other two dams described above, and thousands of feet of dikes, comprise the principal structures of the power project.

St. Lambert Lock.

Cote Ste. Catherine Lock.

Lower Beauharnois Lock.

Upper Beauharnois Lock.

Iroquois Lock, looking upriver. North end of Iroquois Control Dam is shown at left.

The U.S. and Canadian sections of the 3,300 ft. power dam merge at the international boundary near Massena, N.Y. and Cornwall, Ontario.

Not truly a part of the Seaway system, but worth mentioning nonetheless, are two other Canals—the Chicago and the Erie Barge Canal. The latter, which runs 360 miles between Lake Erie and the Hudson River, then to the sea, has from time to time been considered as an alternative route to the sea for the Great Lakes. There are studies now underway by the Corps of Engineers concerning this possibility.

The first Chicago canal was completed in 1848, known as the Illinois and Michigan Canal, it linked the Great Lakes and Chicago with a direct water route to the Mississippi and the Gulf of Mexico. In 1900 the upper stretch of the canal was replaced by a larger Chicago Sanitary and Ship Canal. More recently the entire waterway has been improved: Seven locks were constructed, each capable of handling, at one time, eight giant barges and a towboat, with a cargo capacity of over 10,000 tons. The locks are 600 feet long by 110 feet wide and with a draft of nine feet. In 1964 another addition, the Calumet-Sag Channel was completed, carrying the water all the way up to the deep-draft harbors of Lake Calumet— permitting a Mississippi River access to the vast Chicago ports.

Ocean vessel enters U.S. Snell Lock for up-bound transit.

The mammoth U.S. Seaway gate lifter Grasse River stands ready constantly, a maintenance and emergency device mounted on a barge and capable of replacing the massive Seaway gates. In the unlikely event of a ship breaking a gate, or if other damage occurs, the gate lifter with auxiliary gates is ready to make virtually instantaneous replacement. The photo at right shows the controls of the gate lifter while the one above shows the powerful pulleys and hoists necessary to complete the herculean repair job. The photos at left show views of the gate lifter holding one of the massive lock gate replacements.

Unloading cargo at Duluth.

5

Tolls, Cargo and Operations

How do the Seaway locks work? How does a ship actually climb to the height of a 60-story skyscraper on the water route from the tidewater to the clear, fresh water of Lake Superior? Like this:

All of the locks on the St. Lawrence Seaway are filled or emptied by gravity. To raise a vessel, the upstream valves of the lock are opened and the water simply flows into the chamber through openings at the bottom of the walls. The diagram (below) illustrates the procedure and portrays the following steps.

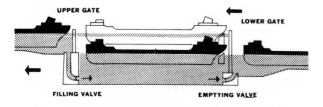

UPPER GATE   LOWER GATE

FILLING VALVE   EMPTYING VALVE

1. From the lower level, the ship sails through the open gates into the lock. The vessel secures itself to bollards on the side of the walls. The gates are closed.

2. The valves are opened and water is allowed to flow in, lifting the ship.
3. When the vessel reaches the higher level the upper gates are opened and the ship sails out.

To lower a vessel the steps are reversed. It takes less than ten minutes to raise or lower the water level of a lock, with more than 20 million gallons used for each lockage. Additional time is required for the vessel to maneuver in and out of the lock chamber. The average lockage requires approximately 33 minutes from the time the bow of the ship passes the approach wall until the stern is cleared of the outermost boom.

SLSDC, as a wholly-owned government corporation created by an Act of Congress, was established to develop, operate and maintain that portion of the St. Lawrence Seaway in the United States territorial waters. Originally a part of the Department of Commerce, SLSDC was later transferred to its more logical position as a modal administration within the Department of Transportation.

It has functioned under four Transportation Secretaries: Alan S. Boyd (1956-1969); John A. Volpe, (1969-1973), Claude Brinegar (1973-1975), and William T. Coleman, Jr. (1975-   ).

D. W. Oberlin has served as administrator under the past three Secretaries. He is the fourth administrator of the Seaway, preceded by Lewis Castle (1954 to 1960); Martin W. Oettershagen, deputy administrator who succeeded Castle upon his death, and served from March to December, 1961; and Joseph McCann (1962 to 1969). Advisory Board members under Boyd were Harry C. Brockel, Milwaukee; Miles F. McKee, Detroit; Kenneth M. Lloyd, Youngstown; Thomas P. McMahon, Buffalo and Martin W. Oettershagen, former Seaway Administrator, Chicago.

Since 1969 Advisory Board members have been Joseph N. Thomas, Gary, Indiana; W. W. Knight, Toledo; Jacob Bernheim, Milwaukee; Dr. Foster H. Brown, Ogdensburg, and Miles McKee, Detroit.

The small town of Massena, N.Y., carries on most of the operational action of the U.S. side of the Seaway. Here, each busy day sees traffic controllers calling the shots as ships ease in and out of the locks, while marine service crews check buoy lights or clear channel obstructions, engineers evaluate new lock flooding systems, and maintenance men track down trouble at a stubborn gate boom.

It's a year-round operation, with winter months calling for repair and maintenance projects of major proportion to keep everything working at the locks.

Nearly 200 floating or fixed aids to navigation are maintained by the Seaway crews: putting them into the water in the spring and decommissioning and repairing them at each season's closing.

Channel maintenance calls for crews to sweep the ship channel to clear it of shoals or high spots, using an electronic sweep system.

Wave heights and frequencies are studied by Corporation engineers on a regular basis, and

Ship's eye view into empty lock at low water.

Lock gates are covered so winter maintenance operations can be undertaken.

A lighted navigation buoy—one of hundreds which mark the channels in the Seaway system.

Control panel at Welland Canal lets traffic control men watch ships as they transit multi-lock system.

because of high water levels, speed control for transiting ships is frequently put into operation to help reduce shoreline damage.

Winter navigation operations (see Chapter VIII) continue during winter months, too, under an ongoing program which SLSDC is conducting in conjunction with a federally funded Winter Navigation Board.

One of the most basic, and yet most interesting activities at Massena, and, of course, elsewhere along the Seaway in the Canadian sections is the actual control of vessels as they transit the system.

Vessel traffic is controlled from three main points. The first, at St. Lambert, Quebec, follows a ship from its entry into the system at Montreal and carries it through four locks to the International Section of the Seaway. Here, at Massena, New York, a second control point picks up the transiting ship and follows it to Ste. Catharines, Ontario, where it is picked up by the third vessel control center and guided through the final chain of eight locks at the Welland Canal. After that, it proceeds into the upper Great Lakes.

When the ship's master "checks in," the ship's name and size are placed on a movable block in a control panel system. As the block travels in sequence "on the board," the ship is watched by closed circuit television, so that in effect the vessel is monitored both in terms of its position in the simulated Seaway line-up and for its own movements.

The traffic control system has already prov-

ed its worth, thanks not only to the system's equipment, but to the 24-hour vigilance of the Canadian and American technicians who make the system work.

The vessel is also in constant radio communication with the control center, normally via VHF radio, although backup support is available with AM radio, radio telephone and teletype.

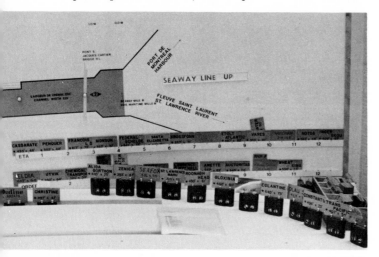

Ships in track at vessel Traffic Control Center.

Another VTC station tracks and charts traffic.

Lineup of ships shows sequence in which ships are transiting the lock system so that no ship gets "lost." System works much on the same principal as that of an airport control tower.

Lockmasters control entrance of ships, open and close gates, control flow of water into and out of lock.

Bridge of laker during Seaway transit.

Passing through Lake St. Louis, a ship enters the Soulanges area, which includes the two Canadian locks, upper and lower Beauharnois.

As a ship approaches Cornwall, it enters the second traffic control unit, this one operated by the United States. Until recently, traffic control operators visually controlled ship transits from towers located at each lock. Now, however, they have the services of closed-circuit television cameras, which provide a greater sweep of the area and a greater feel for the total traffic pattern. As the vessel approaches the Snell Lock it again provides, by radio, its cargo destination and draft. It waits its turn and enters the lock under the radio direction of traffic control, proceeding then to Eisenhower. Following the clearly marked navigation channel, it next enters Iroquois Lock, and then Lake Ontario.

Some 180 miles onward, the vessel arrives at the most dramatic part of the Seaway system: the 28-mile Welland Canal, where eight closely connected locks lift the vessel around the Niagara Escarpment and into Lake Erie.

Here, at Ste. Catharines, the third major traffic control point, closed-circuit television and radio guide ships through the multitude of locks which stair-step the vessel through the last major climb of the Seaway system.

Had the vessel encountered no fog or traffic delays, the passage from Montreal to this point would have taken about 47 hours. Because delays are not unusual, however, actual transit time will probably be longer.

In order to transit the Seaway system, a ship must meet certain requirements. It must, for example, be equipped with VHF radio with prescribed channels and with sufficient power for communicating with Seaway Authority stations from a distance of 30 miles. At various points along the channel, vessels must check in with the nearest control center.

Ocean craft are required to use Seaway pilots during the entire passage. (Masters of lake vessels, intimately familiar with the Seaway and its traffic control system, are not always required to board a pilot.)

Speed restrictions are rigidly enforced.

In addition, ships are required to drop anchor in a dense fog, although the fact that traffic control operates on a 24-hour basis permits nighttime operations in the locks when visibility is normal.

In spite of heavy traffic through the Seaway, accidents in the Great Lakes have been few, with just three sinkings in recent years, one involving a heavily loaded dry-cargo ship which sank after grounding and the second, a collision near the Detroit River. In November 1975, an ore carrier loaded with taconite pellets sank in heavy seas during a Lake Superior storm.

It's pertinent to note here the Seaway's emphasis upon keeping navigation channels clear. If a ship does stray from its channel and goes aground, it must wait to be examined by a Seaway inspector before continuing through the Seaway.

When a ship transits the first of the locks at St. Lambert, a part of the traffic control routine has already been taken care of. The vessel owner or his agent has already filed with the Canadian Seaway authorities a pre-clearance, giving appropriate information on the ship and cargo and agreeing to follow Seaway traffic regulations and of course, to pay the tolls.

The pre-clearance form contains complete identification of the vessel, showing particulars of the ownership as well as physical characteristics. The ship's representative must also guarantee payment of all tolls and provide a deposit or other guarantee to secure the payment of tolls.

The Canadian Seaway Authority is responsible for the billing and collecting of all tolls. Revenue division between the United States and Canada is 73% to Canada and 27% to the United States for a full transit of the Seaway.

Each vessel must also forward a "Seaway Transit Declaration" to the Seaway Authority within 14 days after it enters the Seaway. Verification is made as to the type of cargo carried (bulk or general). In cases of vessels carrying cargo to or from an overseas port, cargo manifests accompany the Seaway declaration. Each manifest is checked for proper classification of cargo and the weight listed. The transit declaration becomes the basis for toll billings.

The toll invoice indicates the amount due to the Canadian Seaway Authority in Canadian funds, and the amount due to the U.S. Seaway Corporation in U.S. funds. Two checks are received for payment of each invoice issued.

For a partial transit of the Seaway between Montreal and Lake Ontario, a vessel pays 15% per lock of the toll that would be assessed if that vessel were to transit the entire Seaway.

The Seaway entities pay all of their operating expenses from toll revenues, returning net operating income—their profits—to their governments to pay for the cost of the Seaway's construction.

Lumber and containers ride side by side on cargo ship.

The Seaway's third administrator, Joseph McCann.

Ship Requirements

TOLLS: MONTREAL TO OR FROM LAKES SUPERIOR OR MICHIGAN

For transit between Montreal and Lake Ontario

There are seven locks in the St. Lawrence River, five in Canada operated by The St. Lawrence Seaway Authority of Canada, and two in the United States operated by the Saint Lawrence Seaway Development Corporation. All locks are similar in size. The specifications are:

Length, breast wall to
gate fender .... 766 feet
(Ships may not exceed 730 feet
  in overall length)
Width............................ 80 feet
Depth over sills .... 30 feet
Locks: .... Lift
St. Lambert................ 13 to 20 feet
Cote Ste. Catherine .... 33 to 35 feet
Lower Beauharnois .... 38 to 42 feet
Upper Beauharnois .... 36 to 40 feet
Snell........................ 45 to 49 feet
Eisenhower .... 38 to 42 feet
Iroquois .... .5 to 6 feet

Locks 1-7 of the Welland Canal are lift locks, Lock 8 is essentially a guard lock. Locks 4, 5, 6 are twinned and in flight. Welland Canal is 27 miles long, overcomes a difference in level of 326 feet, between Lake Ontario and Lake Erie.

The controlling channel dimensions for the Seaway, Lake Erie to Montreal are:

Depth to a minimum of 27 feet—to permit transit ot vessels drawing 25 feet 9 inches (fresh water draft). Width of channel:

(Min.)

When flanked by two embankments 200 feet
When flanked by one embankment 300 feet
In open reaches .... 450 feet

Maximum size of ship permitted to transit the Seaway: Vessels not exceeding 730 feet overall and 75-foot, 6 inch extreme breadth may transit the Seaway. Vessels' masts must not extend more than 117 feet above water level.

In the interest of energy conservation, the first solar powered flasher beacon to aid navigation in the St. Lawrence Seaway has been installed and is being tested by the Seaway Corporation. The beacon is a 300-millimeter, six volt lantern mounted on a fixed platform just above the Bertrand H. Snell Lock. A compact T-module solar cell array converts sunlight or diffuses skylight into a 6 VDC-0.6 amps to charge a lead-acid storage battery package to provide night-time power. Life of the solar array is considered indefinite, with battery replacement expected every 15 years. The Canadian laker "Canadoc" is shown passing Seaway employes installing the beacon.

Before the Seaway, cargoes flowing between the continental interior of North America and the nations of the world were shipped via overland routes to one of three existing coastal ranges. Today, however, vessels which ply the all-water Seaway route deliver midwest cargo directly to ports of the world at a lower cost than do competing land/water routing via tidewater ports.

For instance,

• Shipping earthmoving equipment parts to Antwerp, Belgium, from Euclid, Ohio, through the Port of Cleveland, by container, as opposed to east coast ports saves the shipper $304.50 per container ($17.40/short ton).

• Shipping 5,000 tons of bentonite from Wyoming to the Port of Chicago to Rotterdam, Netherlands, as opposed to shipping from Gulf Coast ports saves $23,350 ($4.67/short ton).

• Shipping plastic granules to Rotterdam, Netherlands, from Midland, Michigan, through Port of Bay City as opposed to shipping from east coast ports saves $35,000 for each 1,000 tons.

• Transporting hand tools by container from Chicago to the mid-European range as opposed to an east coast port saves $550 per container.

Everything that ships by water can fit neatly into one of three categories: general cargo, bulk cargo and—most recently—container cargo.

General cargo includes, by definition, all cargo not suitable for mass mechanical handling or stockpiling. The term incorporates packaged, processed and manufactured products with approximately five times the value per ton of bulk commodities.

The three highest volume years on record for general cargo movement on the Seaway were 1968, eight million tons; 1971, 8.6 million tons, and 1972, 7.8 million tons. Total general cargo traffic culminated during the first 15 years of the Seaway totals 76.3 million tons.

The major components of general cargo on the Seaway are iron and steel products and other manufactured goods. This commodity category now represents over 70% of total Seaway general cargo. Iron and steel movement is primarily upbound, imported from Western Europe and the Far East to the U.S. and Canada.

In contrast with general cargo, which moves primarily in international commerce, the flow of bulk cargo within the Great Lakes far exceeds total bulk and general traffic through the St. Lawrence.

Commerce through the St. Lawrence River section of the System is also dominated by bulk cargoes—ore and grains in particular—which represent about 70% of total Seaway tonnage. Ore shipments through the international section of the Seaway originate in Quebec-Labrador and move upbound to iron and steel producers through off loading ports in Lakes Ontario, Erie and Michigan. The Welland

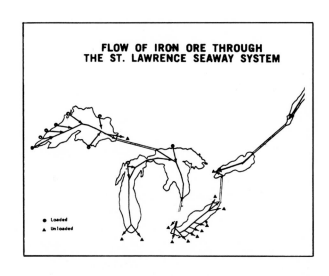

Canal section of the St. Lawrence Seaway has movements of ore in both directions.

Waterborne movement of iron ore within the Lakes is the largest single commodity movement of all Great Lakes-St. Lawrence traffic, accounting for over 45% of all bulk traffic in the System. (The ore movement alone from Lake Superior ports to lower lake ports amounts to something like 80 million gross tons per year.) The other three major commodities in lakes bulk traffic are coal, grains and limestone, in that order.

Lock gates open to permit ship to exit, downbound to the sea.

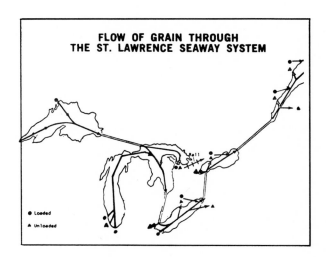

Container is locked up for pickup by crane, which then hoists it to ship's deck.

The movement of U.S. and Canadian grain, notably wheat, corn, soybeans, barley, oats and rye, downbound through the St. Lawrence System accounts for the second major bulk commodity. Grain movements to domestic and export markets provide backhaul cargo for the upbound ore vessels which can return downbound fully laden for all loading at lower ports or downriver St. Lawrence grain ports for the export market.

From the standpoint of total tonnage, coal movement throughout the System is second in importance only to iron ore. The flow of coal is primarily U.S. to U.S. and U.S. to Canada. The coal, used principally for power generation and in steelmaking, flows mostly from the U.S. ports of Lake Erie. The increased movement of low sulphur coal from Duluth-Superior to the lower lakes and in export trade is expected to soon add a new dimension to coal traffic in the System.

Petroleum products moving through the System increased in importance due to the recent energy shortage. Millions of tons of petroleum and related products move through the St. Lawrence River section of the Seaway each year now, with fuel oil as the predominant commodity. The major flow is from Canadian origins to both U.S. and Canadian destinations in the lower lakes.

Coast Guard icebreaker Mackinaw assists ore carrer in ice.

Lake vessel heads into sunset in Straits of Mackinac.

Ore carrier is frosted like a giant birthday cake.
Track of clear water as seen from aft of lakes vessel.

U.S. Steel's Roger Blough at the Soo.

The ocean vessel Zakopne calls at Detroit.

One of five newly constructed Great Lakes & European Line container ships providing major Great Lakes ports with scheduled seven-day container service to the North Europe range.

The Canada Steamship Lines self-unloader Hochelaga.

One day, it seemed, some people had the idea that it would be safer, cheaper and easier if they packed up a lot of general cargo into one big box, locked it up at the port of embarkation, and then shipped to where it was going. Thus was born what they call the container concept—and water transportation has not been the same since.

The container concept unquestionably has created a revolution in the field of transportation and has changed the entire process of waterborne movement of cargoes. (Of course, the conventional breakbulk method of cargo handling is by no means outmoded by containers and the very nature of many products is such that they are not suitable for containerized movement.)

Since 1968, the first year such records were maintained, Seaway container shipments increased from 7,854 units and 85,289 tons to 1972's peak total of 22,478 units and 427,604 tons, a three-fold growth rate in four seasons.

Many maritime experts said that the container movement would seriously hurt the ports of the Great Lakes. But Great Lakes ports quickly responded to the new shipping system by bringing in container equipment and establishing container facilities—notably Duluth, Toledo, Cleveland and Toronto.

In 1968, to encourage container cargoes, empty containers were exempted from tolls in the Seaway. In 1971, a tariff amendment permitted bulk cargo in containers to be charged at bulk rates rather than at general cargo rates, which had been applied to all loaded container shipments. And in 1972, the tare weight of containers was exempted from the chargeable weight of loaded container shipments for tolls assessment.

In 1975 the Great Lakes and European Line (GLE) introduced five new cellular container ships into the Seaway, providing a seven day express container service between North Europe and key Seaway ports. Imaginative, in-

Containers loaded on truck for overland cartage.

Self-unloading container ship.

Containers taken off ship await loading onto truck or rail car.

novative, and well financed, GLE shows promise of becoming the strongest service in the Lakes.

Manchester Liners Ltd. has operated a fully containerized feeder vessel system since 1971 serving lake ports and Montreal. Containers are transferred at Montreal to larger ocean vessels for movement to the UK and other Western European and Mediterranean destinations. Most other carriers servicing the international liner trade provide a mix of containers and breakbulk service on all sailings.

In the mid-70's, responding to a survey by the Great Lakes Commission, ports reported this optimistic response with regard to their container traffic:

Container Cargo Facilities

Port	Facilities
Buffalo	3 berths with adequate support equipment
Chicago	9 berths available with adequate support equipment
Chicago Regional Port District	10 berths available with adequate support equipment
Cleveland	9 berths available with adequate support equipment
Detroit	4 private terminals with 10 berths available with adequate support equipment
Duluth	2 berths—(new 1.5 million container facility just completed)
Erie	7 berths available with adequate support equipment
Port of Indiana	6 berths available with adequate support equipment
Milwaukee	12 berths available with adequate support equipment
Toledo	8 berths available with adequate support equipment
Toronto	5 berths available with adequate support equipment

The visitor never sees the underground equipment needed to open and close lock gates or empty and fill lock chambers.

6

Ports of the Seaway System

The ports had always been there, of course. Some, like Duluth and Detroit and Chicago, had earned rather respectable reputations for their tonnages even before the Seaway was built. Others were content to accept (or at least put up with) what cargoes they could muster from the inter-lake trade: bulk cargoes such as iron ore, grains, limestone, petroleum and chemical products.

The opening of the Seaway and the definition of the System to include everything between Montreal and Lakehead, made a potential international superstar out of each port, or so, at least, each port thought.

There were two schools of thought on port activity, and while both were paid lip service, only one was, in the beginning, actively pursued. The logic went something like this: the more ports that there were to serve, the more ships the Great Lakes would attract. If one port had cargoes, chances are an upbound ship would stop at the neighboring ports too, and perhaps do a little business with them. It was not too far removed from the shopping center theory that all the stores would gain from traffic generated by each one.

And so great waves of conversation dealing with port cooperation and unity swept the system—except that no one really believed that all those theories really meant *their* port. Just the other guy's port. The upshot, of course, was keen competition, carefully guarded secrets of sources of business, mailing lists, and prospective customers.

Today, fortunately, that philosophy does not still hold.

Today there are close to 50 ports on the Great Lakes (see map), each of which is engaged in

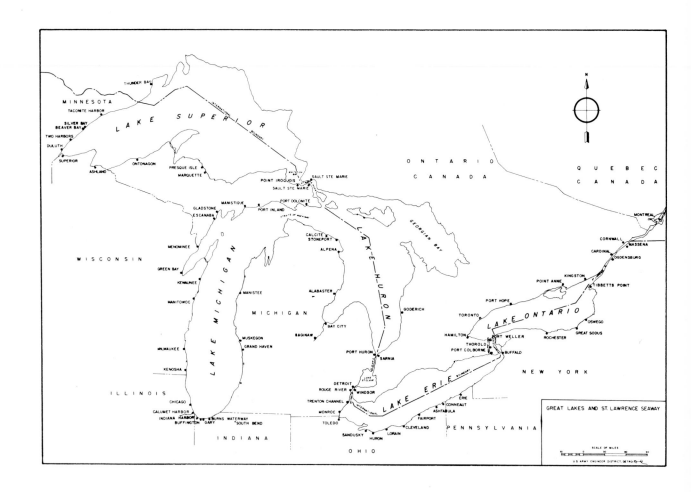

some aspect of intra-lake or foreign commercial shipping. The International Association of Great Lakes Ports (IAGLP) (see Chapter VII) consists of 22 major ports. The St. Lawrence Seaway Development Corporation, in its own system on classification has come up with a tonnage criterion to rank the ports, calling a major international port one which has shipped and/or received a combined minimum of 50,000 tons of non-Canadian import-export cargo per year.

While this listing closely approximates the IAGLP roster, it includes the Ports of Ashtabula, Ohio and Kenosha, Wisc.; deletes the IAGLP ports of Oswego, N.Y. and Monroe, Mich. and separates Duluth, Minn. and Superior, Wisc. into two separate port entities, rather than accepting them as Duluth-Superior.

Today, after the passing of roughly two decades since the establishment of the Seaway, what has happened to the Great Lakes ports and the states they serve?

MICHIGAN

Michigan's strategic location on the Great Lakes is becoming increasingly important as the State continues to claim a significantly larger share of the world's export-import market.

Michigan is the only state which borders four of the Great Lakes, and its 3,200-mile coastline is far greater than any other Great Lakes state. Only Alaska in the U.S. has a longer coastline. All of this gives Michigan the advantage of having its ports along the St. Lawrence Seaway's most-heavily traveled water routes.

Michigan has long been one of the nation's foremost export contributors, and the Port of Detroit, which serves the largest border city in the nation, now ranks as one of the busiest on the continent. Detroit's four ocean-freight terminals passed the 3-million tonnage mark in export-import cargo for the first time in 1971. Detroit, one of four Michigan ports which handle deep draft ocean freighters, is served by many steamship lines. Other Michigan deep-water ports are Port Huron, Bay City, Saginaw and Muskegon, all of which provide ample dockage, material handling, and bonded terminal facilities.

Michigan has taken major steps in recent years to increase its export-import activity, which now averages nearly $5 billion yearly. The State has embarked on a vigorous promotional campaign and has opened overseas offices to help locate and serve new markets for its tremendous annual output of manufactured goods and agricultural products.

Michigan has also currently established its second foreign trade zone at Sault Ste. Marie. Michigan's other facility is at Bay City, which helps provide the nearby Dow Chemical Company plants at Midland with shipping outlets.

Two thousand Michigan firms now engage in world trade, and the number is increasing rapidly. Michigan's leading export items are

Freighters lined up at Detroit.

Loading containers at Duluth. Below, Duluth—Superior Harbor.

motor vehicles and parts, non-electrical machinery, fabricated metal products, chemicals, primary metal products, electrical equipment, and food products. In the latter category alone, the state exports some $115 million worth annually, and ranks third in the U.S. in the export of vegetables to foreign countries.

MINNESOTA

Depending on one's geographic view of things, the Twin Ports of Duluth, Minnesota and Superior, Wisconsin, share the distinction of being at the beginning—or the end—of the St. Lawrence Seaway-Great Lakes system. From either point of view, Minnesota is at the western extremity of the system and, thus,

Calumet Harbor and Navy Pier, (below) Chicago ports.

through its only world port—Duluth—serves a vast Midwestern area extending through the Dakotas, Nebraska, Iowa, Wyoming and Montana.

The common harbor of Duluth-Superior moves more than 42 million tons of cargo during an average shipping season, primarily iron ore from Minnesota's iron range and grain from the port's broad hinterland. More than 38 million tons of import-export cargo have been handled since the Seaway opening, and the port annually leads all others on the Great Lakes in international tonnage.

Grain is the principal export cargo with shipments totalling 8.5 million tons in 1973, a record year for Duluth. The port handles scrap iron and fats and oils in international trade, plus coal, limestone, salt, steel products, gypsum and petroleum products in domestic ship movement.

More than $25 million in public and private funds have been invested in Duluth's port development, including construction of a public marine terminal, a tank farm, a new container facility, a semi-automatic grain elevator (now one of 14 grain berths in the harbor with a total storage capacity of 73.5 million bushels) and a refrigerated storage warehouse.

Minnesota's iron ore shipments via the Great Lakes were over 55 million tons in 1970, 25-30 million of which was shipped to steel centers in the lower lakes area from Duluth-Superior, the nation's leader in this traffic. A rapidly expanding segment of this trade is pelletized taconite ore. In 1971 over 25 million tons of this high iron-content ore was loaded at Duluth-Superior and Minnesota's other major Lake Superior ports of Silver Bay, Taconite Harbor and Two Harbors.

ILLINOIS

Expansion of the role of Illinois in world trade has been materially encouraged by the use of the St. Lawrence Seaway. The tremendous agricultural exports of Illinois, the nation's leader in this field, accounts for its ranking position.

As the major turn-around port of the Great Lakes, Chicago accounts for about one-third of the Seaway's exports and nearly half of the imports. It is reported that annually over 4,000,000 tons of export-import cargo with a value in excess of $500,000,000 are moved through the port.

The Seaport of Chicago is made up of three major terminal centers for international shipping. Navy Pier, the downtown harbor at the mouth of the Chicago River, is primarily a general cargo facility which can accommodate six ocean vessels at one time. This municipally owned lakefront development has more than a half million square feet under roof.

The Lake Calumet area is Chicago's largest ocean shipping development. Some 5,300 linear feet of wharfage and docks along this lake serve a complex of transit facilities, warehouses, grain elevators and storage tanks for fats and oils. This area is also the Great Lakes terminus for barge service which extends from Chicago to the Gulf of Mexico via the Illinois Waterway and Mississippi River.

Chicago's third nucleus of facilities for overseas trade extends along the Calumet River from Lake Michigan to Lake Calumet, and is comprised of terminals handling general cargo, grain and other bulk commodities. The grain elevators located here and in Lake Calumet have a total storage capacity of 54 million bushels and in 1971 loaded over 1½

Port of Indiana at Burns Harbor, on the day it was dedicated in 1970.

million tons (75 million bushels) of grain for export.

The seventeen-state Midwest region served by the Seaway through Chicago accounts for half the nation's agricultural production offered for sale, and 45 percent of American manufacturing value.

INDIANA

The St. Lawrence Seaway is an important factor contributing to the economic advancement of Indiana even though the Hoosier state has a relatively short shore line on Lake Michigan. The industrial developments at Gary, East Chicago, Hammond, Whiting, and most recently Portage, constitute one of the most concentrated industrial regions in the world. Its vast steel mills, oil refineries, cement plants and numerous satellite industries attest to the importance of low cost water transportation.

The new deep-water public Port of Indiana at Burns Waterway Harbor in Portage was dedicated during the Tenth Anniversary Celebration of the Seaway's opening. In addition to being a terminal point for one of the largest steel making complexes in the world, the port serves many other functions for the people of Indiana, and for industries and individuals in a multi-state service area.

Facilities now available include seven modern 27 foot ship berths; plus a mooring facility specifically designed for self-unloader ships; a newly completed modern, heated, sprinkler-equipped transit shed providing 56,-000 square feet of space for general cargo; a prototype waste disposal system second to none in the United States, which handles both port and ship wastes including sanitary wastes, wash and ballast water that may contain oil and various other contaminates. Indiana anticipates that other special facilities will be included as time goes on, such as grain elevators, a refrigerated warehouse, a coal

transfer facility and petroleum service facilities.

The harbor is designed to accommodate the largest vessels operating on the Great Lakes and ocean going ships traversing the St. Lawrence Seaway. These ships are able to enter, berth and depart in minimum time and with little or no tug assistance. Inland waterway barges operating on the Ohio, Mississippi and Illinois River systems enter Lake Michigan via the Calumet River for direct transit to the Port of Indiana-Burns Waterway Harbor.

This modern port, combined with a network of rail, highway, rapid transit, and pipeline facilities, is located in an area widely diversified in agriculture and industry and affords traders of the world an extremely attractive new access to Midwestern markets.

OHIO

Ohio's location on Lake Erie and the St. Lawrence Seaway has provided the State with many trade and transportation advantages. Through capitalization of these advantages, Ohio now ranks third in value added by manufacturing and fourth in exports for the United States. Ohio's central location in America's "industrial heartland" places 60% of the U.S. population, purchasing power, labor force, and manufacturing capacity within 600 miles of the State.

Along Ohio's 200 miles of Lake Erie shoreline have developed four major ports well equipped to handle both bulk and general cargo. These are Toledo, Cleveland, Lorain and Ashtabula-Conneaut.

The Port of Cleveland is actually two ports; one handles the bulk cargoes for Ohio's heavy industry. The other, a public facility, has become the largest overseas general cargo port on Lake Erie. Perhaps because of the importance of Cleveland as a steel and heavy machinery center, this port has a 150-ton capacity (65-foot radius crane) one of the largest on the Great Lakes. Current development plans include for 100% increase in warehouse space to over 500,000 square feet. The marketing potential of 4,000,000 people within 75 miles accounts in part for a 102% increase in net tons of overseas cargo handled between 1965 and 1966.

The Port of Toledo, in total tonnage handled, is the largest bulk cargo port on Lake Erie and is one of the largest in the U.S.A. The railroad complex surrounding the port area is one of the top five centers in the country. The Toledo Harbor features an operating trade zone, one of three in the Seaway system, and is served by a 125-acre, excellently equipped port. Besides coal and iron ore, bulk liquids, grain and general cargoes are the principal commodities annually handled by the Port of Toledo. An increasing number of containers have also been moved through the port's general international cargo complex.

The Port of Lorain, an expanding steel manufacturing center, is assuming even greater importance as a terminal for bulk cargoes of ore, coal and limestone, as well as for

Cleveland harbor from air.

The Port of Toledo's three riverfront grain elevators, Cargill, Inc., left, Mid-States Terminals, Inc., center, and The Andersons, right, established a new export record of over 100 million bushels of grain shipped from Toledo in 1975.

Ashtabula, Ohio.

alloying materials now available from overseas sources.

Ashtabula-Conneaut is well situated to serve not only the heavy industries in the immediate vicinity, but in addition, it provides a favorable gateway to the lighter industries and to the consumer markets of northeastern Ohio.

NEW YORK

New York's extensive frontage on the eastern Great Lakes and the upper St. Lawrence River and the multiple benefits obtained from these vast water bodies have been a major force in the state's economic development. Of particular significance in the commercial growth are the major lake and river ports—Buffalo, Rochester, Oswego, and Ogdensburg. Their locations are most advantageous to provide the northern and western sections of the state with low-cost water transportation. The Seaway-Great Lakes system is an important avenue of trade for the large volume of bulk products handled by the ports. These ports now play an increasingly important role in the world trade of communities in their tributary areas.

The waterborne commerce handled by New York's Seaway ports during the past decade has been highly diversified. The list of exports includes flour, powdered milk, pig iron, aluminum and iron and steel forms and shapes. Included among the imports are iron ore, residual fuels, coal, building cements and pulp.

Buffalo, long a leading Great Lakes port, has some 3½ miles of frontage along its excellent outer harbor. As one of the nation's top milling centers, Buffalo is a large exporter of flour to overseas areas.

The port of Rochester, on Lake Ontario, has developed a substantial volume of overseas general cargo trade since the Seaway era began, and the construction of additional ter-

Vessel unloads gypsum at Buffalo.

Port of Buffalo is primarily a bulk port.

Port of Rochester.

Ogdensburg, New York.

Cranes, cranes, cranes everywhere. Above, Toledo; below, Toronto. On facing page, top left, sketch of new stiff-legged crane at Erie, top right, portable cranes at Chicago, and, below left, another big one at Milwaukee, and right, at Cleveland.

minal facilities at Oswego and Ogdensburg has enabled those ports to accommodate the larger ocean-going vessels.

Benefits from the St. Lawrence Seaway are only beginning to be realized. The Seaway has had a major impact on the state's recreation and tourist business. The U.S. Seaway locks and huge international power dam, constructed in conjunction with the waterway project, are major additions to the entire area.

PENNSYLVANIA

The rapidly growing and well-equipped Port of Erie is Pennsylvania's single port on the Great Lakes-Seaway system, yet it is proving to be of inestimable value to northwestern Pennsylvania. The proximity of the world famous Pennsylvania oil fields together with ferrous and non-ferrous metal enterprises long associated with Pennsylvania and the Allegheny-Ohio River systems have con-

tributed greatly to the growth of the Port. Improvements to the Port of Erie will provide further to Pennsylvania's steel industry both in the handling of raw materials and the exporting of finished steel products.

Exports at Erie are well cared for in 50,000 square feet of storage space under roof. Modern cargo handling methods extend to the oil industry for which unique slings, especially engineered for oil drums, have saved 25% of the loading time usually required for cylindrical loads of this nature.

Heavy earth moving and handling equipment manufactured in the vicnity is handled quickly and safely for overseas shipment.

The Port of Erie, the Commonwealth of Pennsylvania's third largest city, is located on the Southeast Shore of Lake Erie and is in a natural Bay formed and sheltered by Presque Isle Peninsula.

Erie International Marine Terminal, just inside the Harbor, is located on the south shore of Presque Isle Bay, and is owned by the City of Erie and administered by the Port Commission. This is a new location for the cargo pier. Its facilities include a 50,000 sq. ft. warehouse, transit shed and a truck ramp at this shed which can accommodate 20 trailer trucks loading or unloading simultaneously. The Penn Central Co., Norfolk & Western and Bessemer & Lake Erie Railroad service the pier.

WISCONSIN

Wisconsin, with an area of more than 56,000 square miles and a population approaching 5,000,000 people, although known as America's Dairyland, ranks in the top fifteen states in value of manufacturing. As might be expected of a state with 530 miles of shoreline on Lake Michigan and Superior, its largest city, Milwaukee with a population of about 1,400,000 (metropolitan area) is an important port on the St. Lawrence Seaway-Great Lakes system. Wisconsin ranks twelfth among the fifty states in dollar value of exports.

Milwaukee has been unusually far-sighted in its harbor development, and in consequence has been well prepared to serve the growth in Seaway trade which has more than quadrupled since 1959. General cargo, export grain, import steel and heavy-lift machinery have been major factors in this rapid growth. Much of the export movements consist of agricultural implements, heavy construction and mining machinery, electrical apparatus, daily products, flour, grain and cereals, chemicals and oils, edible and inedible paper and forest products.

The city pioneered development of heavy-lift cranes on the Great Lakes. A battery of Gantry cranes, mobile cranes, and locomotive cranes range up to 85 ton capacity. Milwaukee can also boast of a Stiff-leg Derrick capable of 200 net ton lifts, the heaviest on the U.S. side of the Great Lakes-St. Lawrence Seaway. Overseas commerce is in the range of one million tons per

year, and more than fifty shipping lines provide regular service to all parts of the world.

Although Milwaukee is an outstanding port for diversified shipping, including international, excellent harbors have been created to serve Racine, Kenosha, Sheboygan, Manitowoc, Green Bay and Marinette. On Lake Superior, the twin harbors of Superior-Duluth are the largest on the Great Lakes. They are famous for efficient handling of bulk cargoes in tremendous volume, especially iron ore, grain and coal. Manitowoc, Superior, Sturgeon Bay and Marinette are centers for shipbuilding and ship repair.

ONTARIO

The Great Lakes and upper St. Lawrence River form the entire southern border of Ontario and provide the province with an exceptionally advantageous location and potential for economic development. Along this shoreline border lie more than 1,000 miles of deep waterways, extending from the Lakehead (Fort William and Port Arthur) on Lake Superior to Cornwall on the St. Lawrence. This vast resource has contributed in many ways to Ontario's marked economic growth and rise to top position in population.

With over 7.3 million people, Ontario—Canada's industrial heartland—accounts for some 35 per cent of the nation's population and for 46 per cent of the buying power.

The province also is a leader in foreign trade, accounting for 40 per cent of Canada's manufactured goods and 80 per cent of the nation's fully manufactured exports. Access to foreign markets through the St. Lawrence Seaway—via ports such as Toronto, Oshawa, Hamilton, Sarnia, Windsor and the twin ports at the Lakehead—has helped Ontario boast one of the world's highest exports-per-capita figures.

The Seaway's impact is largely on manufacturing and extractive industries. Ontario is Canada's chief mineral-producing province, with the value of production by the mining industry topping the billion-dollar mark.

Largest and most active of the Canadian ports is Toronto. Continued emphasis over the past decade on updating and streamlining marine terminals and equipment has enabled Toronto to offer some of the most modern facilities in the Great Lakes.

Gateway to the largest concentration of industry and population in Canada, Toronto is centrally located in what is called the Golden Horseshoe of Southern Ontario. The port services mainly the heavily populated region adjacent to Lake Ontario from the Niagara Frontier in the south to the Detroit-Windsor

Looking across the Port of Toronto's Container Distribution Center to the city's downtown core. Overseas vessels, berthed at marine terminals 35 and 51 are discharging and loading cargoes. New landmark on the Toronto skyline is the 1,800-foot-tall CN Tower.

area in the west and Peterborough in the east. Goods are also shipped between the port and Canada's Prairie Provinces.

Five marine terminals, owned and operated by the Toronto Harbour Commission, offer 20 berths accommodating vessels of up to maximum Seaway length for both break-bulk and containerized cargoes. There is also a special area for the import and export of motor vehicles.

The port was the first on the Great Lakes to move with the new container concept and provide adequate facilities. The result was the opening of a Container Distribution Centre in 1970.

Since the opening of the St. Lawrence Seaway in 1959, the Toronto Harbour Commission has spent more than $19 million on new terminals and equipment and its general cargo terminals are rated among the most modern in the Lakes.

The area served by any port is known as its "hinterland"—that is, the geographic region which the port can service for its customer more economically and efficiently than any other mode of transportation. If, for instance, a port can accept manufactured goods from a plant 200 miles away and ship those goods abroad more cheaply than the manufacturer can have them shipped by any other mode,

The bustling Port of Milwaukee.

then that plant is considered within the "hinterland" of the port. The same, of course, would hold true for goods being imported.

The Great Lakes-St. Lawrence Seaway system has a vast hinterland, extending to the furthermost borders of Montana, Wyoming and Colorado on the west, Kansas, Missouri, Kentucky on the South, West Virginia, Western Pennsylvania and Western New York on the east, and the greater portions of the province of Ontario, Manitoba and Eastern Quebec on the north.

SLSDC refers to the Seaway hinterland as the system's "Physical Distribution Economy Zone," an appropriate phrase conceived by George E. Wilson, the Seaway's former Assis-

tant Administrator for Development. Goods can be brought in and taken out of this hinterland through the Seaway system at lower costs than via any other mode.

Harry Brockel knows as much about ports as perhaps any other man in America. A former Port of Milwaukee director and early fighter for the Seaway concept, Brockel has noted today that port managements face the problem of adjustment to startling change and to new technologies.

"All forms of transport are being revolutionized," he said. "Port development becomes ever more costly; cost of money is at an all-time high in our history; and cost-benefit ratios become harder to justify. Ports as urban

A sea of cargo awaits shipment from Canada via the Port of Toronto.

Railroad cars loading at Hamilton.

Plastic wrapped pallets are shown here warehoused at Milwaukee, where the unique shrink-wrapped cargo is prepared for international shipment by Hansen Seaway Service. The firm covers pallets with plastic bags, heats them to 350 degrees for 20 seconds, which shrinks the plastic to conform to the outlines of the pallet load. The process prevents pallet loads from coming apart while being shipped, eases loading and unloading, provides safety from weather and discourages pilferage.

Chemicals loading at Bay City-Saginaw.

centers are also storm centers of the environmental and pollution problems. Even routine dredging procedures have become controversial, with public resistance to dumping of silt in open water areas.

"New mechanized cargo handling systems create problems with labor and financing. Maritime labor in all aspects continues to be a problem area. Computer techniques sweep the principal ports. Trade promotion techniques are changing. These are new questions confronting ports all over the world."

Along the Seaway, Brockel noted, lake ports may add to this broad list their own special regional problems: He included these among the problems indigenous to the Great Lakes:

- Hard-core competitive attitudes along the Gulf and Atlantic coasts
- The problem of channel maintenance dredging, capital improvement dredging, and disposal of dredging spoils, as related to the water pollution problem in the Great Lakes
- Rail rate structures favorable to salt-water gateways
- Defense Department resistance to use of lake ports

- Uncertainty as to Seaway toll structures
- Trends to new ships too big for Seaway locks and channels
- Containership competition to Seaway general cargo and probable penetration of lake ports by LASH ship barges, offering through rates from midwestern origins to overseas destinations
- Shippers who resist change, prefer stable year-around shipping methods, or who have a hundred other reasons not to use Seaway routings
- Shrinkage of liner service and sailings into new "consortia"
- Uncertainty as to future attitudes of steamship carriers to raise capital and build ships for a seasonal trade route with special problems
- The changing role of the great connecting canals—Panama, Suez, and the Seaway, particularly.

"Finally," Brockel said, "we have the paradox of a federal government which by law demands the Seaway to be self-liquidating, but which by policy refuses budget resources to promote the waterway. In effect it is saying 'You've got to pay out, but let's not sell the project to the shipping world.'

"To say that port management in this atmosphere must have great expertise, imagina-

Cars awaiting shipment from Toledo.

Green Bay, Wisconsin

tion, promotional skill and high managerial competence, would be laboring the obvious."

Pierre Camu, former Canadian Seaway Authority President, noted that each Great Lakes Port, "has a dual role, a regional as well as an international role. The regional role establishes a rather consistent growth pattern because there are more and more regional activities for the port to deal with. As well, the port serves its immediate hinterland, and develops that end of its business. So it is bound to get increasing traffic.

"I feel that the international role of the Great Lakes and of the Seaway ports is still coming— it's not really here yet," Camu said. "Fifteen years in the life of a port is a very short time, and the Seaway has been open to the traffic of the world for only fifteen years. So now we have growing pains and difficulties. Remember—the true international role of the Seaway ports is still to come."

Maritime students help with the maintenance of the Academy's fleet of ships. Students have scraped and painted all of the Academy's smaller craft, such as the tug, "Captain George," pictured here, in the school colors of red and silver.

Men seeking careers on the Great Lakes can look for help to Northwestern Michigan College at Traverse City, Mich., where the Great Lakes Maritime Academy trains youths for positions of leadership on the inland seas.

While most maritime academies are geared primarily to the ocean going trade, the Great Lakes Academy offers unique opportunities to young men seeking fresh water maritime careers.

On-the-job experience aboard commercial vessels is a part of the course of study that is undertaken at the Academy. The school has its own fleet, too, consisting of a former 143-ft. Navy Pacific fleet tug, the *Allegheny;* a 110-ft. former Coast Guard cutter, *the Hudson,* a 65-ft. tug, the *Captain George,* a 48-ft. harbor tug, the *Anchor Bay,* and such additional floating equipment as work barges, an LCM and sailing sloops.

The curriculum emphasizes a balance of the immediately practical knowledge as well as the academic and theoretical courses. It works to produce a graduate who will have had experience on many kinds of vessels and in many ports of the Great Lakes—a graduate able to cope with most of the skills required in the complex characters of the many ships on the lakes.

7

The Role of Maritime Organizations
in the Great Lakes

Perhaps in no other maritime region of the United States have marine-oriented organizations played a more important role than in the Great Lakes. Special interest groups such as terminals, operators, shippers and labor organizations, geographically structured organizations such as Western Great Lakes and Lake Erie port groups, as well as state-constructed agencies such as the Great Lakes Commission have all played vital and decisive roles in the struggle to help the Seaway system grow from infancy to maturity.

It is sometimes said that there are too many organizations in the Lakes. If this is so, then the useless ones will die off, as they have in the past. But the unity and strength of the maritime system which has emerged from the Seaway's beginnings has, in measure, rested with these groups.

The International Longshoremen's Association, Great Lakes District was active in the Great Lakes long before the opening of the Seaway. ILA represents longshoremen at all ports in the system with the exception of Detroit and Bay City-Saginaw, which are controlled by the Teamsters.

Although a president is elected every four years by the Great Lakes District of ILA, in the Great Lakes the longshore power rests with a scholarly, soft-spoken Buffalo Longshoreman who looks more like a history professor than a labor leader. He is Patrick ("Patty") J. Sullivan, bright, articulate and creative spokesman for more than 120 union locals. Each local represents between 50 and 500 men.

Sullivan has played a major role in the efforts to forge the Great Lakes into a viable, yet cohesive unit. He has earned the esteem of such organizations as The Great Lakes Commission and the Great Lakes Task Force; he is a member of both organizations.

The Seaway Corporation, too, lends a friendly ear to Sullivan, although his efforts to promote a rebuilding of the old Erie Canal as an alternative route to the Great Lakes has raised an eyebrow or two in the system.

Sullivan's counterpart on the fresh water seas of the Great Lakes is Melvin A. Pelfrey, vice president of the National Marine Engineers Beneficial Association (MEBA), the union that represents the rated seamen on the Lakes and signs them up for the duty rosters of the long boats that haul the bulk cargoes of the lakes. Pelfrey was one of the first people to speak out on the human aspects of the Winter Navigation Demonstration Program (See Chapter VIII):

"Labor is not as enthusiastic about sailing ships during the winter season as are the owners or the operators of the ships. There is a saying among people owning ships that a taconite pellet doesn't know the difference between June or January. Let me assure you that the crews on the vessels know the difference between June and January. It is one thing to plan an extended season from a conference room or on a drawing board. Believe me, you get an entirely different perspective from actively sailing on a ship."

Pelfrey, like Sullivan, is soft-spoken and quick to come up with a proposal that benefits not only his own men, but the Seaway system as a whole.

And here, we find one of the great areas of strength in the Lakes today: the fact that labor, while indeed seeking out its own interests, can, and does, work hand in hand with ship owners, ports and terminals for the overall good of the system.

After a recent, particularly bad year for shipping on the Great Lakes resulting from a combination of strikes, the fuel shortage and the high cost of ship charters, labor put together a three-year contract which was a landmark agreement for the system. Sullivan called it, "One of the most significant evidences of labor-management awareness to ever emerge from the Great Lakes—a mutual awareness that we must first agree in order to later enjoy the luxury of being able to disagree."

The contract was unique in several ways including improved regulations dealing with containerization, established specifically to stimulate that trade.

The contract also provided, for the first time, for a joint Union-Management Committee to develop programs to stimulate trade on the Great Lakes.

"The most important factor," Sullivan noted, "is a very real change of attitude on the part of employers and the union membership. There is a new awareness that we both depend on each other for our economic survival and that the

Proclamation of Great Lakes Task Force pledging cooperation to all incoming ships and shippers from all major Great Lakes entities, including ports and labor.

Labor leaders Patrick J. Sullivan, (ILA) and Melvin A. Pelfrey (MEBA)

The Terminals' Thomas D. Wilcox and Harry Brockel, a long-time Seaway fighter.

Task Force chairman John A. McWilliam (Toledo) and past chairman John A. Seefeldt (Milwaukee).

A multi-type cargo vessel.

Members of the International Association of Great Lakes Ports trade missions to Europe on London's Westminister Bridge with Big Ben and the Houses of Parliament in the background. From left, are: Robert Lewis, St. Lawrence Seaway Development Corporation; E. F. Avery, then from the Port of Toledo, now head of the MarAd Great Lakes Regional Marketing office in Detroit; Ian Brown, Toronto; F. D. Flori, then from the Port of Buffalo; S. L. Hamilton, Oswego; W. M. H. Colvin, Toronto; Charles Gress, Windsor; R. K. Jorgensen, Milwaukee; and R. H. Van Derzee, Ogdensburg.

third party—the ship operators—must have our mutual cooperation and understanding."

At the Toledo based MEBA headquarters building, located directly on the waterfront, Pelfrey's people run, among other things, a ships galley and a radar training school. Here, apprentice cooks learn to prepare food for the Great Lakes merchant fleet, called one of the best fed fleets in the world. Stewards, too, learn their trade in a unique operation which culminates in a full-service ship's mess operation, which becomes a cafeteria for union members each day at noon.

Every overseas ship that comes into the Seaway system—with the exception of a few seasoned skippers who know the system like the backs of their hands—must carry, depending upon their destination, either a U.S. or a Canadian pilot to steer them through the locks. The U.S. pilots of District One have an association headed by Anthony (Tony) Rico—Duluth spokesman for the pilots who looks and sounds like the seafaring man he is.

U.S. and Canadian pilots traditionally feud over such things as pay and benefits. Each has its own union representation. A Canadian pilots strike in 1974 brought the Seaway system to its knees—when pilots refused to take any ship through the Welland Canal that was bound for a U.S. port. Although a temporary solution to that particular problem—an armistice really—was hammered out, it took the governments of the United States and Canada to actually work out a settlement under which both highly volatile pilot groups were happy.

The International Association of Great Lakes Ports (IAGLP) is the leading Great Lakes port organization. Founded in 1960, IAGLP consists of 22 major U.S. and Canadian ports, with the president or chairman alternately serving from the U.S. and Canada. It encourages use of the Great Lakes system and works to increase tonnage shipped through lake ports. The Association also plays a role in protecting the best interests of all the ports of the Lakes, not only in terms of cargo, but also in the areas of pollution control, dredging, navigation and local industrial development.

Committee activities in such areas as public relations, legislation and traffic comprise one of the more important functions of IAGLP on the domestic front. Perhaps the most important of these is the traffic committee: Made up of traffic managers from member ports, this committee keeps a close eye on rate structures to insure that coastal ports are not unfairly aided in competing with the Great Lakes for cargoes.

IAGLP regularly conducts overseas trade missions to seek business for the Lakes. In 1973 and again in 1975 it went to Europe to feel the pulse of the overseas market and to induce shipping lines to come into the Seaway system.

The Council of Lake Erie Ports (CLEP) was chartered in 1956, three years before the St. Lawrence Seaway was completed, for the purpose of helping nurture the fledgling waterway. Its membership is largely the 12 ports located on Lake Erie, from Buffalo to Detroit. Membership also includes firms with related interests, such as international banks, freight forwarders, bonded warehouses and shipping agents.

Every year, CLEP holds a meeting to bring together Great Lakes interests in Washington D.C. with Great Lakes Senators and Congressmen, their staffs and other federal officials involved in the Great Lakes. This "Washington Round-up" normally attracts speakers of considerable stature for a morning breakfast. National labor leaders, U.S. Vice Presidents, Cabinet officials and high-ranking Senate and House leaders have addressed the group.

The Great Lakes Task Force (see page 146) participates in the Washington Round-up and normally holds a membership meeting following the breakfast.

Armour S. Armstrong, director of port and intermodal development, U.S. Maritime Administration and leader of an American delegation to Soviet Union, hears about operations in the Baltic Port of Riga from Anatoli F. Poturnak, port director, while other Soviet representatives look on. John A. McWilliam, Great Lakes Task Force chairman and general manager of the Toledo-Lucas County Authority, represented the Great Lakes on the mission, which was sponsored by the U.S. Government.

Great Lakes Commission Seaway, Commerce and Navigation Study Committee in session at Massena, New York, site of U.S. Seaway locks. At left is Brig. General Robert Moore, Chief of the Corps of Engineers North Central Division. Across the table from him is Seaway Administrator D. W. Oberlin (far right), Canada's Seaway Authority President Paul Normandeau and, next to him, Illinois Commissioner, Attorney Warren Jackman. At the far left with arms folded is New York Commissioner and Great Lakes labor leader Patrick J. Sullivan. At podium, Robert Conner, resident manager of the Power Authority for the State of New York, the state agency responsible for the operation of the Moses Saunders Power Dam.

The Western Great Lakes Port Association was formed to promote cargo development of the ports of Lake Michigan. Members include the ports of Chicago, Milwaukee, Green Bay, and Duluth, and the Illinois, Wisconsin and Minnesota Departments of Business.

The Great Lakes Association of Stevedores (GLAS) is the newest of the Lakes organizations. Headed by Chris Kritikos in Chicago, GLAS represents stevedores in Chicago, Duluth, Cleveland, Milwaukee, Burns Harbor, (Ind.), Green Bay, Buffalo, Kenosha, Rochester and Toledo.

The U.S. Great Lakes Shipping Association, includes the following shipping organizations: Blystad, Continental, Fedmar International, Great Lakes Overseas, International Great Lakes Shipping, InterShip, Kerr Steamship, Nordship, Protos and U.S. Navigation.

The organization which has been around the longest, and perhaps which works the hardest for the Lakes is the Great Lakes Commission.

Under the direction of a retired Corps of Engineers combat officer, Col. Leonard J. (Hank) Goodsell, the Commission is a compact agency created in 1955 by the eight Great Lakes States for the purpose of dealing with water resource problems of the Great Lakes and its tributary waters. It is controlled by a group of commissioners—from three to five from each of the eight Great Lakes States.

Five Commission standing committees deal with a parcel of matters ranging from environmental quality control and water

Looking aft

The ice-strengthened 592 ft. bulk carrier Konstantia

Ontario's Premier Davis receives Great Lakes Commission Conservation and Water Management Award from Michigan Governor William G. Milliken at Toronto Conference.

resources, to fish and wildlife activity, water quality and Seaway commerce and navigation.

It is this last area of activity in which the Commission has gained the best part of its well-earned and well-deserved reputation as a watchdog of the Lakes.

Fighting for the benefits of the System, the Commission has established a number of objectives which, through legislative persuasion and downright hard work, it seems to be accomplishing one by one.

The current published objectives of the Commission's Seaway committee include these:

• Increase Great Lakes-St. Lawrence Seaway overseas commerce through continued vigorous legislation, government activities, and administration of cargo preference laws to increased shipments of defense and agricultural cargoes through the Seaway system both in general commerce and under the U.S. Soviet Trade Agreement.

• Eliminate discriminatory inland freight rates for service to Great Lakes ports.

• Implement the Merchant Marine Act of 1970 by establishment of a feeder service from selected Great Lakes ports; fair and equitable regulations concerning administration of cargo preference laws.

• Eliminate the 25% local cost requirement for construction of containment areas for disposal of polluted dredged material.

• Promulgate uniform standards for disposal of vessel wastes.

• Eliminate tolls and user charges on the Great Lakes-St. Lawrence Seaway.

• Study and develop most economical and desirable methods to obtain year round navigation throughout the Great Lakes-St. Lawrence Seaway system, and to serve all waterborne traffic requirements for waterways from the Great Lakes to the sea.

• Re-examination of essential trade routes

into lakes. (MARAD docket S. 173) based on fuel conservation measures, transportation savings, etc.

The Commission holds two meetings a year in which standing committees report on their progress. The meetings, open to the full Great Lakes community, are exceedingly well attended by Great Lakes leadership. Speakers of prominence are invited to bring Lakes leadership up to date on specific areas (such as winter navigation progress, legislative or shipping matters). It is not uncommon to find ranking state and federal officials in attendance either to speak or to listen.

In 1969, the Great Lakes Commission served as the working agency for Great Lakes governors in an international celebration of the 10th anniversary of the Seaway. A 10th anniversary symbol was developed for the effort along with quantities of well-executed informational material for use by ports, schools, governmental units and private citizens.

Every port in the Seaway system held an open house to acquaint its citizens with its importance to the community and its state. At Massena, N.Y. site of the Seaway locks, President Richard Nixon and Prime Minister Pierre Trudeau reenacted the original dedication of the Seaway 10 years previous.

At that time, President Nixon who had, of course, been on hand for the original dedication, called for the realization of the full potential of the Seaway. Nixon also said that the friendship between the two nations was well expressed in the words on the plaque erected when former President Eisenhower and Queen Elizabeth of Britain dedicated the Seaway in 1959:

"Our front is the front of friendship, our ways are the ways of peace, and our works are the works of progress and freedom."

Trudeau responded that, "Good ditches make good neighbors, and the Seaway is truly a marvelous ditch. May that ditch long run between our two nations and insure the friendship of the people of Canada and the people of America."

There are two other commission in the Great Lakes—the Great Lakes Basin Commission, and the Upper Great Lakes Regional Commis-sion. Neither has much to do with shipping matters, although the Chairman of the Basin Commission, Frederick O. Rouse, sits on the Winter Navigation Board and the chairman of the Great Lakes Commission sits as a commissioner on the Basin Commission. The similarity in the choice of names for these groups is unfortunate, and becomes confusing to agencies who are not aware of the widely different roles of the groups.

In August, 1966, the Great Lakes Terminals Association, (GLTA) (see page 148) and IAGLP's traffic committee met in Chicago to discuss common problems. At that meeting they agreed to send a "task force" of associations comprised of members of its IAGLP, GLTA, the Great Lakes Commission and Council of Lake Erie Ports to present the Great Lakes case to the Great Lakes Conference of Senators and other government officials.

Today all of the Great Lakes groups we have examined this far (with the exception of the Great Lakes Basin Commission and the Upper Great Lakes Regional Commission) belong to the Great Lakes *Task Force*.

The *Task Force* works to cut across vested interests and to present a strong, united front for the Lakes. Most of the time, it is effective. The membership consists of *labor,* (International Longshoremen's Association, Marine Engineers Beneficial Association, Great Lakes Association of Stevedores) *ports* (International Association of Great Lakes Ports, Council of Lake Erie Ports, Western Great Lakes Ports Association,) *shippers* (U.S. Great Lakes Shipping Association) and serving both as member and acting as Secretariat, the Great Lakes Commission.

Functioning something like a small-scale United Nations, the Task Force works closely with officials in Washington and the world shipping industry on Seaway matters. Its reputation is especially stong in Europe.

John A. Seefeldt, Director of the Port of Milwaukee and former president of the Task Force, commented upon the group's influence upon returning from a recent trade mission to Europe.

"We were quite surprised to learn that our

Ocean vessels line up to load cargo.

contacts in Europe were following very closely the activities of the Great Lakes Task Force. They knew about Task Force activities in Washington. They knew about Task Force activities to improve the trade on the St. Lawrence Seaway. Ship owners were, in fact, quite conversant with Task Force activities and offered suggestions and comments for future undertakings."

The Task Force, too, has objectives it would like to see obtained in the Great Lakes. The Task Force wishes to:

• Increase Great Lakes-St. Lawrence Seaway commerce through trade promotion, and vigorous legislative and governmental actions to obtain equitable and objective administration of the Merchant Marine Act of 1936, as amended, and establish U.S. flag vessel service into the Great Lakes on a scheduled, convenient basis.

• Eliminate discriminatory inland freight rates for service to Great Lakes ports.

• Eliminate Section 123 (c) PL 91-611 legislation, which requires that non-federal interests contribute 25% of the cost of construction of containment areas for polluted dredged materials and urge the Office of Management and Budget to allocate the full amount appropriated for construction of containment areas.

• Eliminate discriminatory tolls and user charges on the Seaway System.

• Investigate navigation improvements to the Great Lakes-St. Lawrence Seaway System, including alternate routes between the Great Lakes and the sea.

• Encourage international cooperation for environmental conservation and economic development.

At the beginning of the 1975 shipping

Chris Kritikos, head of Great Lakes Association of Stevedores (GLAS) and James Scovic of the Great Lakes-Seaway Industrial Users.

IJC US Chairman Henry Smith discusses Great Lakes water levels with Oberlin and Normandeau, heads of U.S. and Canadian Seaway entities.

season, the Task Force issued a Declaration stating its willingness to help make Great Lakes-Seaway shipping a profitable venture for any overseas shipper coming into the system. The Declaration was carried to Europe by IAGLP members and has been widely distributed in the United States as well.

The Great Lakes Terminals Association brings together the firms which take the cargo off the ships and warehouse it or arrange for its onward transfer.

Internally, the Association provides a forum to discuss problems of stevedores and terminal operators throughout the Great Lakes basin, and the Association has Federal Maritime Commission authority to establish common practices, rules, regulations and terminal charges of Lakes-wide application.

More apparent to non-members is the external activity of the Association as a major proponent of the development of world commerce through the St. Lawrence Seaway ports of Chicago, Bay City, Detroit, Pt. Huron, Rochester, Buffalo, Cleveland, Ashtabula, Toledo, Erie, Green Bay and Milwaukee.

Heading up the group as executive secretary is a well-regarded Washington lawyer by the name of Thomas D. Wilcox, who recently was selected to serve as executive director and general counsel for the National Association of Stevedores.

The terminals were organizers and charter members of the Task Force, but pulled out several years ago and have since gone their own way.

Wilcox tends to be quiet and unassuming, but in defense of the causes he supports, he strikes out with the swiftness and sting of a scorpion, dealing mightily with those who oppose his organization. Needless to say, he is well respected by his peers in the Seaway system.

The Great Lakes fleet of inter-lake carriers is represented by two organizations, the Lake Carriers Association on the United States and the Dominion Marine Association of Canada.

A former Vice Admiral and Deputy Commandant of the Coast Guard, Paul A. Trimble, is executive director of the U.S. organization, while a retired Rear Admiral of the Navy in Canada, virtually a namesake, Robert W. Timbrell is his Canadian counterpart.

The Lake Carriers represent 16 companies who run the 190 ships which comprise the U.S. Great Lakes Fleet, while Dominion Marine represents 18 firms and 150 ships of Canadian registry.

The two groups work closely together in areas of safety, navigation, weather, operation, communications and like matter.

Together, the two organizations represent ships totaling something like 3.2 million gross registered tons.

(A separate book on "The Lake Carriers" is now in process by the author and will be published by *Superior* early next year.)

An orgaization known as the Waterways Development Association, in Canada, works relentlessly toward the elimination of Seaway tolls (see page 181). Headed by a much-admired Canadian, Stuart Armour, the group works consistently to press for the elimination of tolls on the Canadian part of the Seaway system.

The Industrial Users of the St. Lawrence Seaway are also interested in the removal of tolls, although they have other reasons for their organizational being, as well. Formed in 1970 with only 10 members, the organization now boasts over 100 all of whom depend upon the St. Lawrence Seaway system for shipping.

The Industrial Users Group is chaired by an articulate Dow Chemical executive, James Scovic. Also from Dow and also working with the Users is Arthur "Art" Chomistek, who fight the Seaway battles with a special brand of zeal.

The Users want an end to the Seaway tolls. They also want a consistent scheduling of vessels into the system, along with year-round navigation of the Seaway.

Two military services work in the Seaway—the Coast Guard and the U.S. Army Corps of Engineers.

The Great Lakes comes under the jurisdiction of the North Central Division of the Corps, headquartered in Chicago. The Corps is lead agency in the effort to demonstrate the practicability of extending the navigation season on the Lakes into the winter months, when ice normally closes down the shipping lanes. The Board is currently headed by Brig. Gen. Robert L. Moore, a well-renowned, long time friend of the Lakes, and former District Engineer in the Eastern Division of the Corps at Buffalo, N.Y. Before Moore, the Board was headed by Brig. Gen. Walter O. Bachus, a Texan who came into the winter navigation program after it had been underway for three years, under the strong and decisive leadership of Maj. Gen. Ernest Graves. (Corps policy shifts a Division Engineer every three years. Moore took over from Bachus, who took over from Graves. Chapter VIII is devoted to the Great Lakes-Seaway Winter Navigation project.)

The Corps of Engineers also deals with the important matters of harbor and channel dredging—both of vital importance to the Lakes. Because environmental interests have successfully complained about the polluting effects of the disposal of dredge spoils, the practice of the open lake dumping of spoils is no longer possible. For the Corps, this presents a real dilemma.

Dredging is of vital importance to shippers, of course. Without deep channels they cannot haul their cargoes. For every inch deeper it can sink into the the water, an average-size laker can carry over 100 tons more cargo. (A salt water ship entering the Seaway also must take into account the fact that it settles a foot deeper in fresh water for every 36 feet of draft.)

The Corps also functions at the Sault Ste. Marie, as indicated in Chapter IV, running the toll-free locks that separate Lake Superior from the lower Great Lakes.

The Coast Guard in the Great Lakes maintains a well-manned, well-equipped operational organization perfectly suited to supporting maritime commerce. The Guard is organized

Coast Guard cutter Ojibwa (foreground) and Bramble work together in the ice.

The legendary Mackinaw.

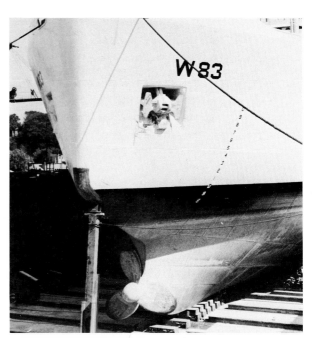

The exposed bow of the Mackinaw shows bow thruster or forward propeller. With two additional stern propellers the Mackinaw uses 10,000 hp to gain top speed of 18.7 knots and can sheer through 4 feet of solid ice or 37 feet of windrow (broken) ice. Vessel can cut a channel 70 feet wide. the 5,250 ton icebreaker has a 1⅝ in. hull plating from keel to above the water line. (See Chapter eight.)

into twelve operational districts; the Ninth Coast Guard District, under the command of Rear Admiral James Gracey, is headquartered at Cleveland and embraces the entire area of the Lakes. The District Commander has at his disposal some 2200 officers and men and 200 civilian employees.

The Coast Guard also maintains six one-hundred-and eighty foot tenders and five one-hundred-ten foot tugs in the Lakes. All of these Coast Guard cutters have icebreaking capability, though they are also utilized for other purposes.

The icebreaker MACKINAW, "Big Mac" as she is called on the Lakes, is two-hundred-and-ninety feet long with 10,000 horsepower. She is capable of punching through solid ice four feet thick and her wide beam clears a path 75 feet

U.S. Navy Destroyer Escort in Seaway locks.

Naval patrol boat right (PTF) and inland shore patrol craft (PCF) left.

wide. The MACKINAW has a heeling system which can transfer a ton of water per second between wing tanks. The rocking motion which results frees the ship from the ice and enables it to back down when beset.

The MACKINAW's bow propeller can force a stream of water from the bow aft to help eliminate the friction of ice along the sides. Or it can be reversed to flush water ahead of the bow and force broken ice from its path. With a draft of just nineteen feet, the MACKINAW can operate easily in most bays and harbors of the Great Lakes.

In addition to these floating units, there are three Coast Guard Air Stations in the Great Lakes area, located at Traverse City, Mich. Detroit and Chicago. Here are stationed eight helicopters and two fixed wing aircraft. Located strategically around the Lakes, the Coast Guard maintains forty-nine stations

A new Great Lakes group, the Chicago Maritime Council works to promote cargo at the Port of Chicago. Executive Director of the group is Vera Paktor.

Penna. Senator Hugh Scott receives Council of Lake Erie Ports citation for his work on behalf of the Great Lakes from Leonard Bolla, Port of Erie, then President of the Association.

engaged primarily in search and rescue work. These stations are a part of an extensive and efficient communication system that is controlled from the District Headquarters in Cleveland.

The Coast Guard also maintains lighthouses and other navigation aids.

Sitting on the Winter Navigation Board, the Coast Guard is responsible for icebreaking assistance to ships and for winter navigation aids.

High in precedence of primary responsibilities is search and rescue, which accounts for nearly half of the Coast Guard's resources.

During the heavy pleasure boating season, May through September, Ninth District search and rescue units handle close to 4,000 cases. To facilitate search and rescue, the Coast Guard uses more than 150 boats of 44 feet in length or less.

To assist the mariner in transiting the proper channels, more than 2,500 buoys and markers have been placed in the Great Lakes and their tributaries. Maintenance and care of these aids is handled by nine Coast Guard buoy tenders which have a unique problem compared to other Coast Guard Districts.

The fact that the lakes freeze in the winter necessitates that all buoys be removed before the heavy ice can set it. During this season, the buoys are repaired and overhauled for replacement next spring.

There are 47 light stations in the lakes manned by Coast Guard personnel, and 584 unmanned stations.

The Coast Guard is also charged with licensing and certifying men aboard America's merchant fleet as well as inspecting the ships and ascertaining that they meet federal safety requirements. Eleven Marine Inspection Offices are located in the lakes to do this job.

The safeguarding of ports is of prime importance, especially during wartime. The division of the Coast Guard responsible for this is the Captain of the Port. Located in Buffalo, Chicago, Cleveland, Detroit, Sault Ste. Marie, Toledo, Duluth, Ludington, Milwaukee and Oswego, Captain of the Port offices make harbor security patrols to insure that ports are safe from accidental destruction in peacetime and purposeful destruction in war.

The story of Coast Guard operation on the Great Lakes would not be complete without mention of the close liaison between Canada and the United States with reference to the Coast Guard's work. International boundaries dissolve when mariners are in distress. Canadian aircraft and rescue ships frequently join in to help Coast Guard operations in American waters, as do Coast Guard facilities help in searches in Canadian waters.

The Navy serves in the Great Lakes, too, although only in a minor way today. Navy ships have normally operated in the lakes, but this activity terminated with the decommissioning of the 9th Naval District Reserve Destroyer Division in 1970. Today, three patrol boats (PFY's) and three inland shore patrol craft (PFCs) are assigned to Naval headquarters at Great Lakes, Illinois.

The FFCs are 51.3 ft. long, weigh 22 tons and have a 25 knot top speed. The PTFs are 80.3 ft. long and weigh 76 tons. Their maximum speed is a very fast 45 knots.

Corps of Engineers dredge barges at work in the lakes.

Coast Guard icebreaker Mackinaw circles ore carrier to break ice in which vessel has become lodged. After breaking ice and freeing ship the Mackinaw will break a track which the ore carrier will follow to open water.

8

Winter Navigation

In the winter months—roughly between mid-December and mid-April—the Seaway system closes down. Or, to put it more properly, the season is *closed* down—by winter, and by the ice that clogs the St. Lawrence River and the constricted channels and ports of the Great Lakes.

The dynamic, vigorous fourth seacost of the United States and the southern coast of Canada, are out of business. The great ports, with their gigantic gantries and cargo moving apparatus, are stilled. The giant, endless warehouses, the terminals are empty. The docks are silent and the slips are glazed over with many feet of ice.

Longshoremen and stevedores and warehousemen, ordinary seamen and sea captains, pilots and port directors are, essentially, out of work: The ships have stopped coming.

The cargo, certainly, may be there, but the ships cannot get to it.

The dilemma of an eight-month shipping season has plagued the Seaway since the very opening of the system. One of the many early arguments that antagonists to the Seaway had used against it, in fact, was that it could not provide a year-round shipping service—that ice would close it down for a good part of each year.

Because ice does close down shipping—interlake as well as international—industries relying upon water transportation for the cartage of bulk cargos are forced to either stockpile to carry them over the winter months, or to have their materials shipped overland, at substantially high rates.

The system, obviously would be more efficient if it could operate year-round—or at least, for a longer period of time.

An investigation into the possibility of extending the navigation season system on the Great Lakes-St. Lawrence Seaway came about as a result of an amendment (Section 107) to the *Rivers and Harbors Act of 1970*. With this legislation, the Congress authorized the expenditure of $6.5 million dollars over a three year period to see if it was feasible and economically beneficial to extend the navigation season in the lakes.

Subsection (a) of the act authorized the Secretary of the Army, acting through the Chief of Engineers, to conduct a survey-scope study of the feasibility of means of extending the season. Subsection (b) authorized the Secretary of the Army' acting through the Chief of Engineers, to undertake a program to demonstrate the practicability of extending the season.

It called for ship voyages extending beyond the normal navigation season; observation of ice conditions and ice forces; environmental and ecological investigations; collections of technical data related to improved vessel design; ice control facilities and navigation aids; physical model studies, and coordination of the collection and dissemination of information to shippers on weather and ice conditions.

In order to accomplish the objectives established by the Congress, a Winter Navigation Board was established to oversee the program.

Chaired by the U.S. Army Corps of Engineers, the Winter Navigation Board consists of the leadership of the U.S. Coast Guard, the St. Lawrence Seaway Development Corporation, National Oceanic and Atmospheric Administration, U.S. Maritime Administration, U.S. Department of the Interior, U.S. Environmental Protection Agency, the Federal Power Commission, the Great Lakes Basin Commission and the Great Lakes Commission.

Technical advisors include the National Aeronautics and Space Administration and the Atomic Energy Commission, with the Canadian St. Lawrence Seaway Authority acting as observer for the overall program. Also assisting the board are observers from the eight Great Lakes states, as well as representatives of both labor and industry.

The investigation has demonstrated that extension of the shipping season in the Great Lakes-St. Lawrence Seaway system is indeed feasible from an engineering standpoint and can produce immense economic benefits for the Great Lakes region and for the nation as a whole with little or no adverse affect upon the environment.

Three realistic options exist for the extension of the navigation season: to January 31, to February 28 or to full, year-round navigation.

The benefit-cost ratio for these alternatives are:

        January 31 .... 5.3
        February 28 .... 6.9
        Year round 7.1

This means, using year-round navigation as an example, that for every dollar spent to achieve the year round shipping objective, seven dollars would be returned.

Translated into dollars, the costs and benefits look like this:

Specific Yearly Benefits (in $1,000)	Season Extension To		
	31 Jan.	28 Feb.	Year round
Total Benefits			
1975	40,283	58,593	68,223
2025	150,674	219,162	247.381
Average Annual Benefits at 5⅝% (discount rate) (in $1,000)	89,723	129,051	146,639
Costs			
Total Initial Investment	184,000	192,000	192,000
Annual Costs at 5⅝% (Interest rate) (in $1,000)			
Interest and Amortization	11,120	11,500	11,500
Operations and Maintenance	5,710	7,090	9,060
Total	16,800	18,600	20,600

Users of bulk commodities (iron ore, coal, stone, grain) which are transported during the regular nine month navigation season now stockpile resources for winter production needs. Savings resulting from a diminished need to stockpile would come from several areas, including interest on capital represented by stockpiled inventory, real estate released for other more productive uses and a reduction in handling costs. The ultimate results of these savings would be reflected in the prices of consumer and industrial goods.

Another area of savings can be found in the utilization of the Great Lakes fleet. An extended season would automatically facilitate the use of newer, more efficient vessels over a longer period of time, as well as result in investments in new vessels and the related, obvious benefits to the Great Lakes ship-building industry.

The expansion and modernization of the American merchant marine in the Great Lakes would also occur, as a result of an extended season, along with more efficient utilization of manpower at shore-related facilities such as terminals, warehouses and overland transportation modes.

Port facilities and locks would also enjoy a broader, more meaningful use as ships would dock during times when, as is now the case, slips are empty for periods of three months or longer.

The greater utilization of port facilities would have strong economic impacts on the port cities, their states and hinterland states.

State unemployment rolls, now increased each winter as the result of Great Lakes port shut-downs, would be automatically reduced as the navigation season was extended.

A 12-month season would add more than $382 million to labor earnings in 11 states by 1980 and one billion dollars by 2020, a report published jointly by The Great Lakes Commission and SEAWAY REVIEW magazine stated. Over 42,000 jobs would be attributable to the total impact on general cargo movement and its associated increase in industrial production.

Economists compute primary income from general cargo $24.00 to $30.00 per ton and $5.00 to $5.27 per ton of bulk cargo. The secondary or indirect income from these types of cargo, as determined by an income multiplier, adds still further to the cargo income. The income multiplier computed for water-borne commerce in the Great Lakes is approximately 2.0. This means that every dollar generated by shipping activity can be doubled when we consider the effect of the income multiplier. If a port, for instance, achieves a direct income of $42 million from shipping, it gains an added $42 million in terms of related secondary befefits for a total of $84 million.

Traffic flow from Europe to the Seaway region has been affected even in summer months because of the unwillingness of overseas shipping firms to plan one course of transportation for their customers during an eight or nine months shipping season and a second course of transportation for the months during which the Great Lakes ports are closed by ice. An expanded shipping season would obviously mean increased shipping during the entire season, in that overseas shippers would be able to route their cargoes at lower cost to port facilities in the lakes on a more or less full-year basis.

George E. Wilson, former Asst. Administrator for development of SLSDC sounded the note of caution that the need for an extended season, possibly year-round, must be considered over the long range as being essential to the national survival of the United States.

"Finland started year-round navigation twelve years ago," Wilson said, "because it was their only alternative to national survival. The Soviet Union, in their national interest, developed inland water transportation to the point that traffic has increased almost 400% between 1941 and 1968, compared with an increase of 120% in the U.S. The Canadians, in their national interest, started in the Gulf of St. Lawrence many years ago," he said.

Canadian winter navigation activities center on improving the operational efficiency of the system. Close U.S. liason with the Canadian Seaway Authority is maintained through intense inter-governmental coordination.

Activities for the first three years of the program have concentrated on the upper Great Lakes portion of the system: In 1973, based upon the successes obtained, Congress appropriated an additional $3 million to extend the test program an additional 2½ years.

Convoy of ore carriers moves through ice.

Before an extended season can be initiated on an operational basis in the St. Lawrence River portion of the system, further experimentation is needed.

One of the Seaway Corporation's efforts in the Season Extension Demonstration Program is entitled the System Plan for All-Year Navigation. (SPAN)

Started in 1973, SPAN is one of the most significant projects undertaken by the Seaway Development Corporation and has been given a major priority in the multi-faceted season extension program.

Essentially, it is intended to identify obstacles to winter navigation on the St. Lawrence River between Montreal and Lake Ontario and make recommendations for priority removal of those obstacles on a cost-effective basis.

Problems in the St. Lawrence arose early in the demonstration program when the New York Power Authority (PASNY) and the

Earlier in the year, Congressmen, government officials and industrial interests visited Finland to study ice techniques and look at the Finnish icebreaking technology. Shown here attending a briefing in the control room of the Urho are (l to r) seated, Former House Public Works Chairman John A. Blatnik; US Ambassador to Finland Mark Evans Austad; Ohio River Basin Commission Fred E. Morr; Asst.Naval Attache of US Embassy in Finland LCDR K. R. Barry; Rep. Philip Ruppe (R-Mich.); Great Lakes Basin Commission Chairman Frederick O. Rouse; St. Lawrence Seaway Development Corporation Administrator David W. Oberlin; Wartsila Company President Tankmar Horn, US Embassy Naval Attache CDR. Lowell D. Dahl and Managing Director of Wartsila Shipbuilding Christian Landtman.

Seaway Development Corporation (SLSDC) bumped heads over the rights to use the water.

Primary obstacles to an extended navigation season on the St. Lawrence are ice booms installed across the river each year by the power entities at Ogdensburg-Prescott, Galop Island and in the Beauharnois Canal (see sketch).

The purpose of the ice booms is to assist in the formation and maintenance of a stable ice cover during the winter. Such an ice cover is required in order to maintain the flow capacity of the river—a highly important consideration for control of the level of Lake Ontario, for power generation at the Moses-Saunders Power Plant in Massena-Cornwall and down-river at the Quebec-Hydro plants near Montreal.

Two of these booms cross the Seaway navigation channel and, as James A. FitzPatrick, Chairman of the New York Power Authority

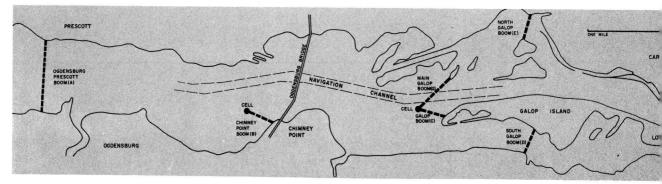

Locations of ice booms along the Seaway.

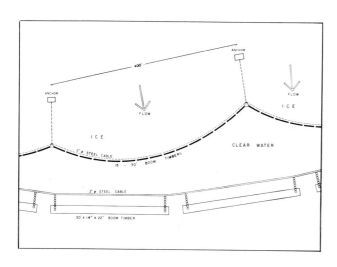

Drawing shows construction of ice booms.

Each winter, ice booms such as the one shown in this aerial view are placed across the St. Lawrence River by the New York Power Authority. The booms are used both to accelerate the formation of ice and to stabilize the ice cover, thus insuring a continuing, reliable flow of ice for the power generators. The booms have been an impediment to winter navigation in this part of the Seaway System.

noted, a shipping season extended into the ice-forming period would require that the ice booms remain open.

"This would immediately result in reduced flows down the river, thereby disrupting the plan of regulation for Lake Ontario, reducing the power output of the Authority's plant as well as the plants of Ontario Hydro and Quebec Hydro, and causing flooding upstream of the jam itself.

"Before proceeding with ice breaking experiments that may produce serious damage to other interests on the St. Lawrence River," he added, "those involved should recognize and assert their willingness to shoulder full legal and financial responsibility for the effects of such experimentation . . ."

What had been called the "ice boom dilemma" has become for SLSDC and the Winter Navigation Board a challenge. The problem, simply stated, was this: how could ice booms best be modified to allow for winter navigation, while still maintaining the stability of the ice cover and the hydraulic integrity of the river?

SLSDC took important steps towards solving the problem at the Copeland Cut section of the St. Lawrence River. Here, SLSDC constructed a test ice boom with an opening in the boom which allowed a ship to pass through it without affecting the integrity of the ice cover. SLSDC demonstrated in model tests that after the ship passed through the boom the broken ice would form a bridge above the opening in the boom and naturally begin to consolidate. The princi-

ple was demonstrated inadvertently on January 27, 1975 when an ice boom at Ogdensburg broke and the broken ice immediately began to form a bridge, and consolidate naturally above an opening in the boom which had developed when the boom separated.

The Copeland Cut Test Ice Boom trial showed that ships could indeed transit the ice fields and still allow the booms to maintain the

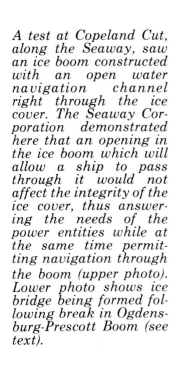

A test at Copeland Cut, along the Seaway, saw an ice boom constructed with an open water navigation channel right through the ice cover. The Seaway Corporation demonstrated here that an opening in the ice boom which will allow a ship to pass through it would not affect the integrity of the ice cover, thus answering the needs of the power entities while at the same time permitting navigation through the boom (upper photo). Lower photo shows ice bridge being formed following break in Ogdensburg-Prescott Boom (see text).

A piece of bubbler pipe. Air is forced through small hole in pipe which is anchored at the bottom of a channel. Compressed air is pumped through pipe and emitted from holes which forces warmer water to surface to impede freezing.

Coastguardsman sets up lights to permit icebreaker to work at night.

Navigational aids shown above have been pulled from channels for winter.

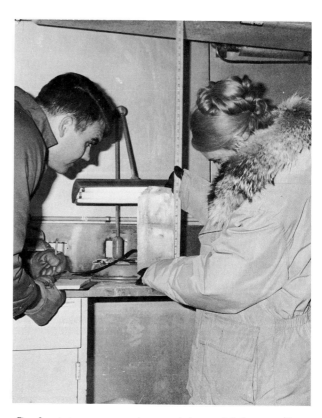

Geologists cut sections of ice which are then polished and examined with polarized light.

Ships in ice.

stability of the ice cover and the hydraulic integrity of the river.

Among the dozens of techniques being utilized in the demonstration program to aid ship transits of ice covered waters are new ice navigation concepts and systems, advanced weather forecasting systems, new ice control techniques, intensified ice-breaker assistance and the use of bubbler systems, which bring warmer below-surface water to the surface to minimize ice coverage.

Thus far, the demonstration program has shown us a great deal. As Professor John A. Hazard reported in a study prepared for the Michigan State Chamber of Commerce and funded by that organization, along with the St. Lawrence Seaway Development Corporation and the Great Lakes Commission, "Ice is not a monolithic obstacle to be overcome by sheer brute force of icebreaking but a subtle natural phenomenon to be managed by a combination of techniques . . .

"Ships," Professor Hazard noted, "venture out to meet the rigors of winter navigation primarily because of fuller utilization of the more efficient ships in the fleet and stockpile savings to the users. The number passing through the Soo after December 15 has increased from 40 transits carrying 400,000 tons to 763 transits carrying 9.1 million tons."

He pointed to subtle lessons in managerial economics arising out of the Winter Navigation program:

"The task force approach evolved by the Winter Navigation Board is the most effective mode of organizing and managing a season extension effort. It harnesses the combined skills of several federal agencies, regional, state and local port interests, and private industry and shipping, and brings them effectively to bear on the diverse functions that must be performed. It also incorporates environmental groups in the early planning and avoids disabling litigation later on . . ."

Professor Hazard astutely noted that a serious error in strategy "may have been to ask for too little funds ($6.5 million) and time (four years) to complete the systemwide demonstration. The 'Catch 22' paradox of small projects more successful than anticipated is that they are frequently treated the same as large projects with cost overruns. Thus, the request for extension of time and funds," he said, "was held to eighteen months and $2.2 million . . . Better strategy may have been to request ten to fifteen years and sufficient funds to carry out the systemwide demonstration."

Season extension is an important initiative for year-round navigation, Hazard has insisted, but other elements of the Great Lakes-St. Lawrence Seaway will "have to be upgraded and improved in their own right and progressively geared to year-round operations." He included these elements:

• Ships will have to be ice strengthened and equipped, expand their service offerings, and regularize their operations.

• Ports will have to be geared to all-weather operations, expand their facilities, and up-date their services at key load centers.

• Inland carriers will have to gear their operations, rates and services to the expanding potentials of an all-weather trade route.

• Shippers will have to alter their logistics, warehousing and distribution practices to take full advantage of an expanding Great Lakes Seaway service.

"It is noteworthy", Hazard concluded, "that the major initiative and expenditures for all of these elements must come from within the region rather than be borne at the federal and dominion levels".

Although money is authorized for a federal project, getting it can sometimes be a problem. Once authorized, it must then be approved once again in the form of an actual appropriation. Often a public works project can be approved, but money for it fails to be appropriated, effectively killing the project.

Seeking appropriations for the Great Lakes winter navigation demonstration effort, sixteen senators, led by Senator William Proxmire, sent this communication to the Senate Appropriations Committee:

"Extension of the Seaway navigation season offers a number of long-term benefits. For instance, a recent study conducted by the University of Wisconsin Center for Great Lakes Studies indicated that only a six-week extension of the navigation season would result in gross benefits of nearly $500,000,000 in less than 10 years.

"One of the top labor officials of the Great Lakes District of the ILA, Mr. Patrick L. Sullivan, has pointed out some of the benefits to labor from an extended season.

"Many longshore jobs require a high degree of skills and semi-skills. Because employment is restricted to eight or eight and a half months, some of these men leave the industry to seek permanent employment, or the stevedore employer subsidized them with make work during the off season, thus increasing costs. Having a longer season with more work opportunity, the turnover, particularly with trained, skilled, men would lower."

"Furthermore, Secretary of Transportation John Volpe has stated in an article in *SEAWAY REVIEW* magazine that "any enlargement of Seaway capacity—through extending the season, for example—would contribute more to the economic well-being" of the Midwest area—an area which he notes is suffering from economic erosion.

"Congress has committed itself to exploring the potential of an extended shipping season on the Great Lakes and the St. Lawrence Seaway, and many public and private groups have joined forces in an unprecedented degree of cooperation to implement that policy . . .

"To make next year's program meaningful the Corps of Engineers must have funds to operate at full capability. We therefore request that your Subcommittee approve the full $3,535,000 to carry forward the season extension program for the Great Lakes and the St. Lawrence Seaway."

s/William Proxmire (D-Wis.)
    Phillip A. Hart (D-Mich.)
    Hubert H. Humphrey (D-Minn.)
    Robert Taft, Jr. (R-Ohio)
    Gaylord Nelson (D-Wis.)
    Walter R. Mondale (D-Minn.)
    Birch Bayh (D-Ind.)
    Robert P. Griffin (R-Mich.)
    Vance Hartke (D-Ind.)
    Hugh Scott (R-Pa.)
    Charles H. Percy (R-Ill.)
    Richard Schweiker (R-Pa.)
    William B. Saxbe (R-Ohio)
    James L. Buckley (R-N.Y.)
    Adlai E. Stevenson III (D-Ill.)
    Jacob K. Javits (R-N.Y.)

Stockpiling helps industry meet needs of a nation until the shipping lanes open in the spring.

The bridge of the icebreaker, Edisto.

Here's what the Great Lakes Governors say about extending the shipping season on the Great Lakes:

Wendell R. Anderson,
Governor of Minnesota

Milton J. Shapp,
Governor of Pennsyl-
vania

Patrick J. Lucey,
Governor of Wisconsin

Otis R. Bowen, M.D.,
Governor of Indiana

James A. Rhodes,
Governor of Ohio

Hugh Carey,
Governor of New York

William G. Milliken,
Governor of Michigan

Dan Walker,
Governor of Illinois

Winter navigation is vital to an expanding world market. Our region's vast production ability could be greatly enhanced with an extended shipping season through Minnesota's world seaport at Duluth.
—Wendell R. Anderson, Governor of Minnesota

The effort to entend the winter navigation season on the Great Lakes-St. Lawrence Seaway is a logical step toward the greater utilization of this vital waterway. A year-round shipping season would have a tremendous economic impact upon all Great Lakes ports.
—Milton J. Shapp, Governor of Pennsylvania

As the supply of energy becomes increasingly uncertain, the need for efficient and environmentally sound transportation advances becomes even more important. Extension of the Great Lakes shipping season is one area that could be properly explored in that context. More intensive and extensive use of our nation's fourth seacoast merits careful attention. But care needs to be taken to insure that all environmental and safety concerns are carefully researched and taken into account
—Patrick J. Lucey, Governor of Wisconsin

Twelve months navigation on the Great Lakes would bring added traffic worth millions of dollars to Indiana and thus provide more stability for the economy of the midwest.
—Otis R. Bowen, Governor of Indiana

Two of the major variables in the price of products today are the cost of the energy to produce the product and the cost of transportation of the raw materials and finished products. Extension of the Great Lakes-St. Lawrence shipping season would help minimize both costs to the benefit of both the industry and consumers of the Great Lakes states. Thus Ohio enthusiastically supports the efforts to extend the shipping season of her Great Lakes ports.
—James A. Rhodes, Governor of Ohio

Extending the length of the shipping season would lead to more efficient utilization of manpower and facilities at New York's Great Lakes ports. These efforts must include provision for maintaining flows for hydroelectric energy generation and must protect shorelands and other environmental resources.
—Hugh Carey, Governor of New York

I believe that full-year navigation of the St. Lawrence Seaway promises expanded opportunities for the marketing of Michigan products to the world. In fact, all the states and provinces which are located on the Seaway will benefit from continued development of the Seaway's potential.
—William G. Milliken, Governor of Michigan

For every month added to the Great Lakes shipping season it is calculated that $20 million will flow directly and indirectly into the economy of the State of Illinois. Such benefits are essential and must be realized with no significant adverse environmental effects in the System.
—Dan Walker, Governor of Illinois

9

Ships of the Seaway System

With a volume of over 7,000 ships passing through the Seaway each year, (a figure which includes about a thousand private pleasure boats) it seems only logical that every once in a while a ship would come through that really caused some excitement, even among the old hands at the locks.

"You'd be amazed what we see coming up the canal sometimes," a lockmaster remarked. "Sometimes I can't believe my eyes."

Strange ships, different ships, ships that confound or amaze—they all seem to make their way into the Seaway.

. . . Like the time just half-a-ship came through the locks. This was hull no. 1173, the bow of the supership, a 1000-foot laker which was to be completed at American Shipyards at Lorain, Ohio. The bow, manufactured in Mississippi, sailed under her own steam up the Atlantic seaboard and through the Seaway, where she was joined to the remainder of the ship, never to leave the lakes again. (A waggish shipyard crew had painted a dotted line and the words "Cut here" on her aftersection.)

Then there was the time a replica of a 19th century ketch, the Nonesuch, sailed into the lock for a lift into the lakes.

One of the more welcome sights in the locks has been the return of the scheduled passenger cruise ships, long absent from the Great Lakes.

"People on decks, waving and cheering, a band playing, flags and lights ablaze—a shipload of happiness—that's a great sight to see in a lock," a lockmaster said.

At one time, the gleaming white cruiseship was a familiar sight on the Great Lakes. Cruise ships such as The Theodore Roosevelt, The

United States, the North America, and South America and the Alabama used to regularly ply the scenic routes of the lakes. And all of the great romance of the sea was there: the russet moon, the lapping of the water against the hulls, the dance music and the cool night sea breezes as the steamers worked their way leisurely from port to port.

The last of the great lines died in 1969 when the Duluth, Chicago and Georgian Bay Line, (DC & GB) operator of the North and South America, went out of business with the enact-ment of federal safety-at-sea legislation. The new marine safety laws called for the extensive rebuilding of older passenger ships, looking to potential fire hazards in, especially, the wooden cabins of the steamers. With the retirement of the North and South America, passenger service on the Great Lakes simply died.

In the early 1970's there was talk that one of the Norwegian Caribbean liners, the sleek, saucy vessels which ply the sunshine route every winter, might consider coming into the

The ketch Nonsuch sails into Seaway locks. The ship is a replica of an 18th century vessel.

Half a ship enters the Seaway under the designation, Hull 1173. Known at the time as "Stubby" the better half of a Great Lakes 1,000 foot super vessel was built for land-locked use in the lakes. The bow came into the system under its own power.

The stately queens of another era put up for winter.

The "United States" off Saugatuck, Michigan.

Car ferries extend U.S. route 10 from Ludington across Lake Michigan to Manitowoc, Wisconsin where the interstate highway continues to the west coast. The car ferries also carry railroad cars.

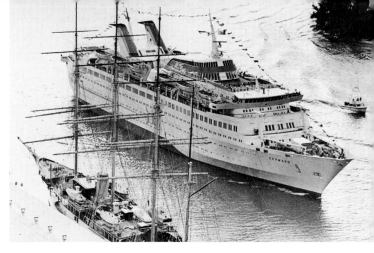

The William R. Roesch was designed specifically to navigate the turns of the Cuyahoga River without the use of a tug. Built by an American Shipbuilding Company at Lorain, Ohio, she became the first American Great Lakes vessel with the wheelhouse and super structure set aft.

Sleek Norwegian cruise ship more typical of "come back" of cruise business in the Lakes today.

The Federal Atlantic Lakes Line Great Lakes container ship.

A once common sight on the Great Lakes was the Whaleback, commonly known as the pig boat because of its snub nose. Shown above is the Meteor sailing in the automobile trade in the early 30's. This old timer is now retired at the Port of Superior in a permanent berth in front of the Douglas County Historical Society Museum.

The Stewart J. Cort, another 1,000 landlocked super laker carries 50,000 tons of iron ore pellets from Taconite Harbor, Minn. to the Bethlehem Steel at Burns Harbor, Indiana. The Poe Lock at Sault St. Marie is the only one in the Seaway system capable of handling the new breed of freighters.

system for summer cruises. But nothing materialized, although independent and knowledgeable inquiries were made by Erwin J. Goebel, former owner of the DC&GB Line, and by editors of *SEAWAY REVIEW,* the Great Lakes maritime magazine.

In 1974, the first cruise ship in many years entered the lakes under a foreign charter, and worked through a fairly successful season. In 1975, Midwest Tours out of Indianapolis chartered a Danish registry ship, named it the Lowell Thomas Discoverer, and launched a renewed high-quality scheduled liner service for passengers between major Great Lakes ports.

The Hercules Scan, a unique self unloader.

Nearly 90% of the lake commerce consists of the movement of bulk commodities such as iron ore, coal, grain and limestone. This has led to the development of a unique type of vessel, designed specifically for the handling of bulk cargo.

The design of the Great Lakes bulk cargo ship is peculiar to the Great Lakes. These ships, from the smallest to the largest, are similarly constructed with bridge and deck crew houses forward and engine and boiler spaces and the engineers' crew house in the after end. The intermediate portion of the ship, devoted entirely to cargo, is provided with athwartships hatches permitting the entire deck to be thrown open to the reception or discharge of cargo.

The ships have double bottoms for the carriage of water ballast and for safety in the event of bottom damage. They are also equipped with side tanks which, in addition to the purposes served by the double bottoms, give the cross-section of the cargo hold a hopper shape that facilitates cargo handling.

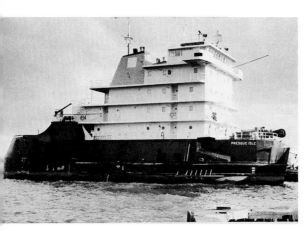

The Presque Isle a 1,000 ft. integrated tug barge which combines a 975 ft. barge and a 153 ft. pusher tug. The tug (below left) fits comfortably into a notch in the stern of the barge (below right). The tug has a special hull configuration which locks it tightly into the structure of the barge.

Floating dry dock at Detroit above enables ship repairs to be made in the Seaway system. Shipbuilders in the Lakes—and there are many—also handle ship repairs.

The 324 ft. self unloader Yankcanuck.

Loading cargo onto modern ocean vessel.

A busy harbor.

Giant laker emphasizes bulk loading equipment.

The Seaway Queen—a very familiar vessel in the system.

Ship at grain elevator carries camouflage markings from a less peaceful era.

10

The Cry Against Discrimination

The eight Great Lakes states which surround the Seaway system contain 37% of the population of the United States and pay over 40% of the nation's income taxes. Over 80% of the population of Canada lives in the region served by the Seaway. Forty-two percent of the industry of the United States is located in that region. The largest exporting states in the U.S. are located here.

In 1959, these states, Wisconsin, Minnesota, Illinois, Indiana, Ohio, Michigan, Pennsylvania and New York were provided with a modest public improvement—modest in terms of similar improvements which have been provided elsewhere in the nation. This was the St. Lawrence Seaway.

They were also given the bill.

The Seaway became the only waterway in the United States (or Canada, for that matter) which had been improved by the federal government, and was then told it had to pay back the cost of its improvement. The reason, of course, goes back to the old railroad, private utility, East and Gulf Coast port pressures. In the final stretches of Seaway legislation, proponents for the waterway had to promise a pay-back to the government in order to obtain passage for any kind of a Seaway construction bill at all.

The logic of the situation, of course, was that payback meant tolls, and tolls meant that the Seaway would be less of a threat to the other modes, since shippers would have to pay to use it. The bill was $124 million of capital debt, plus interest, payable to a federal government which historically had provided toll-free port and waterway improvement since the founding of the Republic. For instance, the federal government in the mid-60s appropriated $1.3 billion on a non-reimbursable basis to improve the Red and Arkansas Rivers in much the same way the St. Lawrence was improved.

As Chairman of the Special Subcommittee to study transportation on the Great Lakes-St. Lawrence Seaway, Senator Vance Hartke (Ind.) called the contrasting treatment accorded the St. Lawrence and the Arkansas River projects a "blatant example of the continuing discrimination which the Seaway has confronted.

"Historically," Hartke said, "it has been the policy of the United States to build and maintain waterways out of general revenues. No other federally supported waterway in America charges tolls or is required to repay its cost of construction.

"The longstanding policy of toll-free waterways was deviated from in the case of the St. Lawrence Seaway because of the political pressures of Eastern shipping interests and other political pressure groups. There is no reason in logic or equity for this discrimination. In addition to the Arkansas River project, one can cite numerous other waterway projects which are not required to amortize the cost of their construction or even pay the cost of their operation and maintenance.

"For example, the Delaware River Channel was constructed at a cost of $130 million and its operation and maintenance has amounted to an additional $140 million—all of which was paid out of general revenues.

"The justification for constructing and maintaining other waterways out of general revenues is that they produce benefits to the general public and not just to the user.

"In that regard, a study by the Federal Maritime Administration indicates that the Seaway has resulted in additional income of $300 million per year to the population of the Great Lakes States, *a 200% annual return on the original investment* which must certainly

Four Seaway fighters: Senators Robert P. Griffin, upper left, Philip A. Hart, lower right (both of Michigan), Walter F. Mondale, Minn., lower left and William W. Proxmire, Wis., upper right. Sen. Proxmire is Chairman of the highly influential Great Lakes Conference of Senators.

Minnesota Senator Walter F. Mondale (l.) and Indiana Senator Vance Hartke appear in Duluth with Port Director C. Thomas Burke for Senate Commerce Sub-committee hearing on Great Lakes-Seaway transportation.

compare favorable to the public benefit resulting from other waterways."

Also speaking out against tolls, Michigan Senator Phillip A. Hart noted that "The only 'rationale' for tolls—and it's a fundamental one—is that the present method of financing the Seaway was forced on the supporters to obtain passage of the legislation authorizing its construction.

"The discrimination is written into the law," Hart said.

"No other river or harbor improvement—including the Red and Arkansas Rivers project—has been burdened with this requirement. There is no justice to it, but those who placed the yoke on (the Seaway) are no weaker or less determined now than they were then."

The primary objective of all Great Lakes organizations, from the Great Lakes Commission, the grandfather of them all, to the Great Lakes Task Force, which includes port, labor and shipping interests (See Chapter VII) has been to rid the Seaway of the burden of tolls.

Col. R. Wilson Neff, former director of the Port of Lorain (Ohio) and in 1970, President of the Council of Lake Erie Ports, put it as well as anyone: He said the tolls were first and foremost among the "goblins" which had discouraged capital investment and vessel services needed to realize the full potential of the Seaway.

"The first priority item (for us) must be elimination of the tolls," Neff said. "If this isn't done, then every coastal port that has received federal public works money for deepening, dredging and so on, should be required to pay for navigation improvement.

"Absurd, you say: of course it's absurd, but let's use the same rules for everyone.

"The tolls," he said, "were injected as a political compromise that was necessary to obtain the Seaway legislation and they short change 65 million (sic) people in the Great Lakes-Midwestern area from receiving the full benefits of a new transportation connection to the oceans of the world."

He noted that the midwest is the largest exporting area in the nation, and that "the people have a right to be indignant when false

It was the floor ammendment of Hugh Scott, shown here with Administrator D. W. Oberlin, which made the Merchant Marine Act of 1970 a reality, as far as the Seaway was concerned. Scott's ammendment gave fourth seacoast status to the Great Lakes and eliminated interest on the Seaway construction debt.

transportation costs are injected into the system that can give them the most economical service."

What does Canada say about tolls?

Canada's prestigous Stuart Armour, President of Great Lakes Waterways Development Association, has noted that "There are 27,000 miles of navigable waters in North America. Of that mileage all are free of tolls of any kind except the 124 miles of the International St. Lawrence Seaway from Montreal to Lake Ontario, and the 27 miles of the all-Canadian Welland Ship Canal.

"You may ship overseas cargoes from or to any of Canada's Arctic, Atlantic or Pacific ports without paying for the privilege," Armour has said. "But you cannot do so from or to any Canadian or United States port on the Great Lakes without paying cargo and ship tolls on the Seaway and/or vessel lockage charges on the Welland Ship Canal.

"It is, of course, very difficult for Canadian users of the Seaway to comprehend the attitude of our Government toward that vital facility," he noted. "For after all, we constructed on our own, and at our own expense operated and maintained an all-Canadian Seaway from Montreal to Lake Erie without tolls for one hundred and eleven years before the present

Dr. John Hazard, (then) Asst. Secretary of Transportation for Policy and International Affairs, addresses maritime interests at Detroit during winter navigation seminar.

At Saranac Lake, New York, an August, 1970 meeting of Great Lakes leaders gave impetus to the establishment of the federally funded Season Extension Demonstration Program. The informal conference was sponsored by the U.S. Seaway Corporation to establish objectives for the waterway system. Speaking, at rear, is Thomas D. Wilcox, Great Lakes Terminal Association executive secretary and highly regarded Washington attorney.

Great Lakes Waterways Development Association

Alberta Wheat Pool—Calgary
Algoma Central Railway—Sault Ste. Marie
Blenkhorn & Sawle Limited—St. Catharines
The Board of Trade of Metrolpolitan Toronto — Toronto
Bowaters Mersey Paper Company Limited— Liverpool, Nova Scotia
Bunge Corporation Limited—Winnipeg
Canada Steamship Lines, Limited—Montreal
Canadian Co-Operative Wheat Producers Limited— Regina
The Canadian Fuel Marketers Group Ltd.—Toronto
Cargill Grain Canada Ltd.—Winnipeg
The Chamber of Commerce Niagara Falls, Canada—Niagara Falls
Continental Grain Company (Canada) Limited— Winnipeg
Dominion Foundaries and Steel, Limited—Hamilton
The Greater Port Colborne Chamber of Commerce— Port Colborne
The Greater Welland Chamber of Commerce— Welland
Gulf Oil Canada Limited—Toronto
Hamilton and District Chamber of Commerce— Hamilton
Hindman Transportation Co. Ltd.—Owen Sound
Hollinger Mines Limited—Toronto
Hollinger North Shore Exploration Company Limited—Montreal
International Harvester Company of Canada, Limited—Hamilton .
Iron Ore Company of Canada—Montreal
Labrador Mining and Exploration Company Limited—Toronto
Lakehead Terminal Elevators Association— Winnipeg
Louis Dreyfus Canada Ltd.—Winnipeg
*Manitoba Pool Elevators—Winnipeg
Captain F. Manzzutti—Sault Ste. Marie

Maple Leaf Mills Limited—Toronto
E. G. Marsh Ltd.—Port Colborne
Misener Enterprises Limited—St. Catharines
The North-West Line Elevators Association— Winnipeg
The Ogilvie Flour Mills Company, Limited— Montreal
The Ontario Paper Company Limited—Thorgold
Palliser Wheat Growers Association—Regina
Papachristidis Shipping Ltd.—Montreal
N. M. Paterson & Sons Limited—Thunder Bay
Port Weller Dry Docks Limited—St. Catharines
The Proctor & Gamble Company of Canada, Limited—Toronto
Quebec North Shore Paper Company—Baie Comeau, Quebec
Regina Chamber of Commerce—Regina
James Richardson & Son, Limited—Winnipeg
Robin Hood Multifoods Limited—Montreal
Rochester & Pittsburgh Coal Co. (Canada) Limited— Toronto
St. Catharines & District Chamber of Commerce— St. Catharines
*Saskatchewan Wheat Pool—Regina
Sault Ste. Marie & District Chamber of Commerce— Sault Ste. Marie
Scott Misener Steamships Limited—St. Catharines
The Shippers & Exporters Association of the Winnipeg Commodity Exchange—Winnipeg
The Steel Company of Canada, Limited—Toronto
Thorold Chamber of Commerce—Thorold
Three Rivers Elevators Ltd.—Trois Rivieres
Thunder Bay Chamber of Commerce—Thunder Bay
Trans-Lake Chartering Ltd.—Winnipeg
Upper Lakes Shipping Ltd.—Toronto
Victory Soya Mills Limited—Toronto
Westinghouse Canada Limited—Hamilton
*Members of Canadian Co-Operative Wheat Producers Limited—Regina

181

William H. Kennedy, St. Lawrence Seaway Development Corporation Resident Manager, and George E. Wilson, former Assistant Administrator for Development, are interviewed by WWNY-TV newsman Joseph Mittiga during media inspection of the Seaway.

International Seaway became fully operational in 1959.

"We did this at great cost because the St. Lawrence River affords Canadians their only feasible water transportation route into the Great Lakes. It is one of our greatest misfortunes that we do not have the vast network of inland waterways which serves the United States population so efficiently."

Questioning the actual legality of tolls, he reminds Canadians that "In our Seaway Act of 1951, our Government made this declaration: "Nothing in this Act affects the operation of the Canada International Boundary Water Treaty Act."

The Boundary Waters Treaty states in its preamble that: "Navigation of all navigable Boundary Waters shall forever continue free and open for the purposes of commerce to the inhabitants and to ships, vessels and boats of both Countries."

Eastern rail carriers and the tidewater ports, those continuous antagonists of Seaway construction, feared, back in the days of legislative battles, that Great Lakes cargo diversions would have a serious effect upon them. Studies have reported to the contrary, that only modest diversions have occured, and in spite of the Seaway, both have consistently carried substantially heavier cargoes than before the Seaway was constructed.

Yet, today, believe it or not, the railroads are still fighting the Seaway. Rail rates to and from Great Lakes ports for commodities shipped in foreign trade are substantially higher than rates for these same commodities shipped for domestic consumption.

To state it very plainly, the International Commerce Committee (ICC) has been accused by Congressional leaders and Great Lakes interests of discriminating against the midwest and the ports in the Great Lakes.

Electrical transformers made in Zanesville, Ohio, for example, can be shipped all the way to the Port of New York for export for less than

Benford and key members of the Marine Transport Economics Team.

The University of Michigan's Department of Naval Architecture and Marine Engineering has developed for the U.S. Maritime Administration a versatile technique for predicting by computer the economics of almost any sort of ship or barge that might operate through the Seaway. This includes vessels that would become feasible only if the Seaway locks were enlarged or channels deepened.

A Marine Transport Economics team, headed by Professor Harry Benford created and designed the unique computer program.

In the case of ships engaged in moving bulk commodities through the Seaway, the computer shows that year-round navigation would allow savings of up to 12.5 percent in required freight rates. Even larger savings could be effected by moderate deepening of the system and a major enlargement of the locks. For example, a 1200-ft by 150-ft bulk carrier with 28-ft draft could effect savings of 38.5 percent over ships of the current maximum size (730 ft x 75 ft x 25.75 ft).

Computer projections also show that a well-designed Seaway feeder service could offer unitized cargo freight rates between 25 and 50 percent lower than those currently charged by the railroads. If the shipping season were extended to 350 days per year, the rail rates could be beaten by 40 to 65 percent.

The most attractive vessel for the Seaway feeder service would appear to be a LASH type ship carrying 20-ft containers in standard lighters. Although a tug-barge container could offer slightly lower required freight rates, it would be at the cost of discouragingly long delivery times.

Important economic gains would result from any changes leading to quicker turnaround times for ships using the Seaway, the computer's program indicates. Fewer delays, faster locking procedures, and shorter times in port are all worthwhile objectives. In the case of unitized cargo, if current port times could be halved, required freight rates would be reduced by 22 percent.

Factors offering the greatest benefits to Seaway commerce are greater allowable ship size (for bulk carriers), extension of operating season, and reduction of turnaround time.

they can be shipped to the nearby Great Lakes port of Cleveland.

"This is the type of rate discrimination which is handcuffing the development of our ports and our international competitive status," says U.S. Senator Robert Taft, Jr.

In 1971, Herbert O. Whitten, a transportation consultant for the Department of Transportation estimated that:

There are in existence 43 trillion railroad rates on file at the ICC. "I have personally measured the tariffs on file in the ICC tariff room and counted 4,300 feet of tariffs—without an index to the rates covered."

Whitten said, "This is equal to a stack 7½ to 8 times as tall as the Washington Monument or 3-2/5 times as tall as the Empire State Building with its TV antenna.

"Interestingly enough some 1,300 electric utilities manage to produce about twice as much revenue in the same national economy with a rate structure which is entirely contained in a book about 2-2/5 inches thick, published by the Federal Power Commission."

Senator Taft tells one classic story regarding the freight rate jungle:

"One only has to think of the Hilt truck line which became so frustrated at ICC practices that it filed a tariff (a price for shipping) on yak fat from Omaha to Chicago.

"If there are any yaks in the United States, I have never seen one. But the tariff stated that the yak fat would be shipped in minimum quantities of 80,000 pounds and would be acceptable in glass or metal containers, barrels, boxes, pails or tubs. The Western

Seaway Corporation headquarters at Massena, New York.

Railroads became so alarmed that this rate might take all of the yak fat business away from them that they requested the ICC to suspend the yak fat rate. The railroads filed documents which purported to show that yak fat hauling costs added up to 63 cents a hundred pounds and therefore the 45-cent rate of the Hilt truck line would be below cost!

"The regulatory process had become such a never-never land that the non-existence of yak fat freight did not slow up the ICC at all. On April 7, 1965, the ICC's Board of Suspension voted to suspend the yak fat rate.

"By mid-April the ICC received a letter from the railroads stating that they had formed a committee to argue the yak fat case, which committee included the Burlington, the Rock Island, Chicago Great Western, the North Western, the Illinois Central, and the Milwaukee Road."

And that's only one story.

"How frustrating it must be," Senator Taft noted, "for directors of Great Lakes ports to know that they must not only develop port facilties, but must fight against their own federal government in seeking to use their ports.

"These discriminatory policies, if permitted to continue, will mean that every year, thousands of jobs are lost to the economies of Great Lakes communities in favor of the Atlantic ports.

"Today, rail rates vary not only by commodity but also by the direction in which the freight moves," Senator Taft notes. "An importer of sugar in Columbus, Ohio, could have it shipped to his place of business more cheaply by rail from Norfolk, Va., than from next door in Toledo. A buyer of chrome ore in Calvert, Ky., could have it shipped to him from New Orleans for about one-third as much as from nearer-by Toledo.

"To ship synthetic rubber from Louisville, Ky. to New York for export, 834 miles, the rate in 1970 was 95 cents per hundred weight. But the rate for the same commodity to Toledo, a distance of only 298 miles was $1.18."

Why it should cost 23¢ more per hundredweight to ship synthetic rubber 536 less miles is a secret locked within the bureaucratic jungles of the ICC.

U.S. Senator Robert Taft, Jr. of Ohio, follows in the footsteps of his equally well known father. An avid Great Lakes supporter, he has long fought against rail inequities.

When the cost of getting the product from the manufacturer to the market can be reduced over 200%—for a new savings of something like 15% of total retail price—that's news for both the buyer and the seller. International Sports Corp. of Cleveland imported these skis from Marsailles via the Seaway at a cost of .84 per pair, total shipping, compared to $2.96 for air shipment. The difference in transport time was only 11 days.

Despite inequities, Great Lakes ports have prospered, but many congressional officials indicate, they have reached only a fraction of their full potential.

At right, Railroad car empties by unique device which locks boxcar and tilts it into storage unit for dumping. Same thing happens to truck below.

Historic photo shows President Richard M. Nixon signing 1970 Merchant Marine Act which gave Fourth Seacoast status to the Great Lakes and eliminated past and future interest on Seaway construction debt.

11

The Oberlin Years

It wasn't until after the first ten years had passed that the Seaway finally began the real process of maturity. The first decade of operation had seen growth, to be sure, but the level of growth came nowhere near living up to the promise which had been so optimistically predicted for the waterway.

After getting off to a flying start during its first years, the lethargy that became so evident in the later part of the Castle Administration carried through the Oettershagen and the McCann years, and seemed to become the dominant pattern of the Seaway. The pattern seemed to be, *don't cause any trouble—don't make any waves. Just lock the ships through— that's what the job is all about.*

Discrimination, obviously an ongoing problem for the Seaway and the Great Lakes ports, has not been restricted to tolls and rate inequities. The persuasive pressures of the traditional Seaway foes extended from special interest groups to lobbies to Congressional offices to federal agencies. But fortunately,

many of the battles which have been fought with relentless and dogged determination by Seaway and Great Lakes supporters, have been won. And all of these victories—splendid triumphs won against the same kind of overwhelming odds and monied pressures which have characterized the Seaway's struggle since its conception—have been achieved under the administration of the stalwart and subtly aggressive Seaway champion, David W. Oberlin.

When the first Nixon Administration came into power, the question, of course, was who Nixon would appoint to be the new Seaway administrator. McCann, a Kennedy Democrat, had tendered his resignation, and it had been accepted. A career civil servant by the name of Brendon T. Jose, deputy administrator under McCann, had been named acting administrator until a Presidential appointee was named. And so the word went out from Republican Washington to the Lakes: Who would be a good man for the job?

Four names were eventually put forward—Harry Brockel, the former Milwaukee port director and old Seaway promoter who had fought so hard for the waterway in the early days—Brockel, who served on the Seaway Advisory Board, and who had earned a reputation of calling the shots as he saw them. Another name put forward was the tough infighter and Washington sea lawyer, Tom Wilcox, head of the Terminals Association.

Out of Columbus, Ohio, Gov. James Rhodes sent forth the name of George E. Wilson, his former state Director of Development—a professional development executive with a consistent track record of success both for himself and for the State of Ohio. Wilson, at the time, had left state government and was now working as a consultant for John Volpe, the new Secretary of Transportation.

Out of Duluth came the recommendation of a port director by the name of Oberlin. David W. Oberlin for two years had functioned as port director at the Seaway Port of Duluth, coming to the post from Toledo, where he had served as assistant secretary and fiscal officer for the $70 million Ohio port. Tenacious, hard working, but good humored and well liked in the system, Oberlin got the nod first from the Great Lakes Task Force and ultimately from the Great Lakes Conference of Senators and was tapped for the job. He accepted. Wilson agreed to accept the number two post as Assistant Administrator for Development, a post he held until mid-1975.

But who was this man Oberlin? What kind of a man was he? According to a Toledo associate, Robert J. Mey, former public relations director for the Toledo-Lucas County Port Authority, Oberlin was "posessed of an insatiable appetite for devouring the impossible.

"Dave Oberlin," Mey said, "has a very effective formula for solving problems. He looks at all four sides of a situation at once, then takes action in all directions at the same time."

A Navy combat veteran of World War II—Oberlin was a submarine torpedo officer—he holds an engineering degree from the University of Michigan.

His appointment as Seaway Administrator was announced by President Nixon just before he addressed the nation from Massena, N.Y., home of the Seaway Development Corporation, during the tenth anniversary of the Seaway. And when the President said he wanted the Seaway to achieve its full maturity, the words became a mandate for the new administrator.

Oberlin set out to achieve this objective. By "attacking all sides of the problem at once," he concluded that the logistics of Seaway operation were all wrong. It was just fine to be based in the attractive Seaway headquarters building at Seaway Circle, Massena, N.Y., when it came to the day-to-day operational aspects of the Seaway, but this was no place from which to operate for the good of the system.

The epicenter was wrong. So he moved himself and a few key people smack into the middle of the Department of Transportation at 800 Independence Avenue. And he put out the shingle to announce to official Washington that the St. Lawrence Seaway had come to town.

(At Massena, a force of about 170 engineering and administrative personnel, along with lockmasters and lock tenders conduct quite effectively their day to day duties of letting the ships pass, without Oberlin just as he had predicted. Today, a tough, well-liked government career officer, and former Marine sergeant, William Kennedy, surpervises the Massena operation as Resident Manager and Assistant Administrator.)

Once in Washington, Dave Oberlin set out to sell his Seaway. Undoubtedly his most important accomplishment was to create a political awareness for the Seaway system that had never existed before. "Political awareness" is a rather pat phrase; behind it had to be hundreds of hours of hard and dedicated work to make the Seaway known and to create new legislative recognizance of its problems and its goals. He began to become involved. Official

Washington began to hear about this Seaway. With the staffs of Great Lakes Senators and Congressmen, and with the Congressional leaders themselves, he began to rekindle legislative fires. Soon they began to ask questions, help him seek solutions to his well defined problems. Maritime Administration and Maritime Commission officials, important legislative committees (like the House Public Works Committee) began to know that there was something going on in the Great Lakes.

Oberlin became deeply involved with the Great Lakes Task Force, an organization he credits with laying much of the groundwork for his later efforts in Washington. He put Wilson to work establishing the highly effective Office of Systems and Economic Analysis, as part of his development program—an investigative, evaluative and predictive arm of the Corporation.

Under the original Seaway act, the Corporation was not permitted to advertise or promote itself in any way—another ridiculous restraint that has been placed upon the Seaway by its opponents.

Oberlin countered that ruling: "If we can't advertise the Seaway, we sure as hell can educate the world about it," and within a

Two University of Michigan alumni meet: President Ford greets Oberlin shortly after the Nixon resignation.

matter of two years, cargo reached heights which had been predicted—but had never ever been achieved before. The years 1971, 1972 and 1973 saw record tonnages—over 50 million tons each year pour through the waterway.

The basic problem—that of paying back the debt for the Seaway's construction—remained the biggest problem in the Oberlin Administration.

The Seaway paid its own way, of course, with all operating and maintenance expenses coming out of user charges. But the interest on the Corporation's debt was so staggering that SLSDC could barely pay that.

The government, in fact, had been issuing 3% loans to non-profit corporations while it was charging the Seaway Corporation—its own agency—6¼% for renewable bonds.

As Michigan's Senator Philip Hart noted, "It is difficult to understand why the Seaway should be charged high interest rates while the Department of Agriculture is making long-term loans for golf course construction at three per cent."

There were other problems, too. Minnesota's Senator Walter Mondale said that he found it "appalling that approximately 35% of the material exported by the Department of Defense originates in the Great Lakes states, but less than .01% of it is shipped through Great Lakes ports."

"What this all means," he said, "is that, in spite of our hard won gains, in spite of the continued pressure of the Congress, and in spite of the hopeful prospects, the Great Lakes are not yet an equal partner in our nation's transportation system."

The St. Lawrence Seaway Development Corporation Advisory Board meets with Corporation officials in Massena to discuss current Seaway matters. Shown left to right are William H. Kennedy, SLSDC resident manager; Dr. Foster H. Brown, Board member, of Ogdensburg, N.Y.; George E. Wilson, former Assistant Administrator for Development; Brendon T. Jose, one-time Assistant Administrator; Joseph N. Thomas, Board member of Gary, Indiana; David W. Oberlin, Administrator; Frederick A. Bush, General Counsel; William W. Knight, Jr., Board member of Toledo, Ohio, and Jacob L. Bernheim, Board member of Milwaukee, Wisconsin. Miles McKee, also a member of the Advisory Board, was unable to attend. Photo was taken in 1973.

Fighters for the Fourth Seacoast legislation in both the Congress and the Executive branch of government are all smiles after the passage of the legislation. Shown left to right are Seaway Administrator D. W. Oberlin, Michigan Senators Robert P. Griffin and Philip A. Hart, Rep. John A. Blatnik, Minn., John A. Volpe, former Secretary of Transportation, Rep. Ancher Nelson, Minn., and John D. Dingell, Mich.

The Seaway, indeed, suffered a country-cousin status in terms of the other coasts of the nation. The opening of the Seaway had, of course, created a fourth coastal range for the United States, and while everyone was aware of it, no one in Washington's maritime circles bothered to officially acknowledge it.

Then too, the three tidewater coastal ranges had regional Maritime Administration offices located on each of the coasts—East, West and Gulf—while there was none on the Great Lakes.

There was an absence of American flag vessels in the Lakes. All of the business that was being conducted in international trade was being carried by foreign flag vessels. This meant, too, that Great Lakes ports could not

qualify for Department of Defense or Department of Agriculture cargoes because the law stipulated that these cargoes had to be carried on U.S. flag vessels.

In turn this meant that while the Great Lakes region manufactured great quantities of the military production of the nation, not one ton of it could be shipped out of Great Lakes ports. Rather, it had to be transshipped overland by rail or truck, and picked up by American flag vessels at the tidewater ports.

Perhaps the most pressing of the problems of the day was that of the Seaway debt. Fifteen Great Lakes Senators had jointly introduced legislation to wipe out the debt completely, making the Seaway responsible only for its operational and maintenance costs—that is,

Senator Hugh Scott and Congressman John Blatnik co-authored legislation in support of continuation of the winter navigation demonstration program.

paying its own way completely, but being relieved of the problem of debt reimbursement.

This legislation failed.

However, thanks largely to the efforts and legislative skill of Pennsylvania's Senator Hugh Scott, a floor amendment to the Merchant Marine Act of 1970 at least cancelled the crippling interest payments on the Seaway construction debt.

The enactment of the Scott amendment did not come easily. It represented, in fact, the successful conclusion of a long and uphill fight to beat back the opposition of key Maryland members of Congress who—with the Eastern port of Baltimore in mind—had used their positions in the past to block Seaway legislation.

Leaders in the battle against Seaway relief had been Maryland Senator Joseph D. Tydings, a ranking Democratic member of the Senate Commerce Committee, and two extremely powerful Democratic members of the Maryland delegation to the U.S. House of Representatives—Congressman Edward A. Garmatz, Chairman of the House Committee on Merchant Marine and Fisheries, and Con-

gressman George H. Fallon, Chairman of the House Committee on Public Works. Both Congressmen were from Baltimore.

And there was another problem.

Cargo volumes which were less than predicted levels, along with unanticipated expenses for repairs to Seaway locks had placed the Seaway under severe financial pressures. With no financial relief in sight, toll increases on the St. Lawrence Seaway were viewed as virtually inevitable. The Seaway's opponents were, of course, not at all unhappy with the prospect of a toll increase.

Working quietly behind the scenes, Scott's people took the Seaway's case directly to the White House.

The result, after extensive negotiations, was an announcement on August 10, 1970, by U.S. Transportation Secretary John Volpe that the Nixon Administration had adopted a position officially opposing any increase in Seaway tolls. The announcement said the Administration would make this possible by submitting to Congress legislation to cancel immediately $22.4 million in interest on the St. Lawrence Seaway debt as well as all other interest

DOT Secretary John A. Volpe swears in D.W. Oberlin as Administrator in 1969.

DOT Secretary William Coleman, Jr., swears Oberlin in for new seven-year term in 1975.

Another Transportation Secretary tours the Seaway, Claude S. Brinegar.

otherwise payable to the U.S. Treasury under the terms of the original legislation creating the Seaway.

The ultimate savings to the Seaway was calculated by Transportation Department officials at more than one-half billion dollars.

Normally, new bills require the approval of the committees to which they are referred in the Senate and the House. In the Senate, the Seaway bill would go to Sen. Tyding's Commerce Committee.

Scott came up with a strategy to bypass the Senate Commerce Committee and the certain opposition of Tydings by offering the bill as a floor amendment to the Merchant Marine Act, which had already been reported out of the Commerce Committee and which was then awaiting floor debate.

As the Senate Minority Leader, Scott was in an ideal position to carry off this maneuver on

the Senate floor. He did, and the Senate accepted his St. Lawrence Seaway provision on a 56-14 roll call vote—adding it as an amendment to the Senate version of the Merchant Marine Act.

But the battle still wasn't over.

Because the House-passed version of the Merchant Marine bill contained no similar provision, the Seaway amendment was referred to the Senate-House Conference Committee named to resolve differences between the two chambers and to write final provisions of the Merchant Marine Act.

Heading the House delegation to the Senate-House Conference on Sept. 29 was Baltimore Congressman Garmatz, whose Committee in the House had been responsible for handling the Merchant Marine Act. Garmatz might have succeeded in killing Scott's seaway amendment had the House delegation not included, as another Democratic member, Congressman Frank M. Clark of Pennsylvania's 25th Congressional District.

Scott talked with Clark, argued that the amendment was good for shippers and others who depend on the St. Lawrence Seaway for jobs and for a viable transportation alternative.

Clark agreed with his Pennsylvania colleague and led the fight against Garmatz that saved the Scott amendment in Conference. When the final version of the Merchant Marine Act was reported from Conference back to the Senate and House on October 7, it contained the Scott St. Lawrence Seaway amendment, without change.

The basic purpose of the Merchant Marine Act of 1970 was to authorize the Administration's $1 billion program for the construction of 300 new ships in American yards, to revitalize the U.S. Merchant Marine.

As passed by the House, the original bill would have excluded Great Lakes shipping from participation in the new program. This was corrected with three additional amendments to permit Great Lakes shipping to participate equally in the new Act with other forms of shipping. Scott, as a member of the Senate Commerce Committee, supported these amendments also.

Andrew E. Gibson, then Federal Maritime Administrator, called the Merchant Marine bill "landmark legislation."

"We now have on the books, for the first time, a bill that fully recognizes the St. Lawrence Seaway as the nation's fourth seacoast," he said.

With the interest on the debt removed, the Seaway had a chance, at least, of paying back the principal of its obligation to the government. And the legislation that wiped out the interest on the debt at the same time erased pressures on the part of the Seaway's opponents—still strong and still there—for higher tolls which, in itself, would have created adverse effects upon the midwest.

Transportation Secretary John A. Volpe, in supporting the legislation had written to Congress in 1970 that the amendment would "put the waterway on a sound, long-term footing and permit the Seaway Corporation to effectively develop the movement of cargo through the Seaway.

"The law will help rectify many of the injustices that Great Lakes shipping and Great Lakes commerce has endured for years," he said.

Oberlin noted that, "last year alone (1969), the Seaway transported well over 41 million tons of cargo, in the face of an iron ore strike

First American flag in the lakes since the mid 60's—Lykes Line at Detroit.

SLSDC Comptroller Edward Margosian presents to Administrator Oberlin the first of two $1,000,000 for the Seaway's bonded debt, representing the first million dollars to be paid to the U.S. Treasury for the cost of the Seaway's construction.

early in the season. Some 6,300 ships transited the Seaway, returning over $5.9 million in revenue.

"It cost us $2.2 million to operate the system. Depreciation for the year stood at $1.7 million, and lock rehabilitation, executed on a reimbursable basis to the U.S. Corps of Engineers, cost us $3.5 million. When you add to this nearly $6 million owed in interest charges, you end up with a $7.4 million loss.

"When interest on your loan costs you nearly three times as much as it does to operate your business, you are in trouble," Oberlin said. "And this has been the plight of the Seaway since it was dedicated over 11 years ago. You can see why I am obviously pleased that this unrealistic burden has at last been erased. Now we can get down to the business of running a profitable operation, and of returning to the Treasury the money we owe it."

And so the Seaway began a program of repaying its obligation to the Treasury, instead of simply paying interest.

The legislation that erased the debt interest also solved some other big problems for the Seaway. Primarily, it officially and for the record granted seacoast status to the Great Lakes. The Great Lakes Task Force and Great Lakes Commission along with a lot of other people, had been fighting for this kind of legislation for a long time: It meant several good things for the system.

In the words of Michigan's Senator Robert Griffin, "The Act amended the existing law, the Merchant Marine Act of 1936, to permit operators of the Great Lakes fleet to enjoy the same privileges with respect to tax deferrals and government-aided ship construction that have long been available to ocean carriers.

"The 1970 Act also contained a provision that contracts entered into under the 1936 Act shall be entered into so as to equitably serve the foreign trade requirements of Great Lakes ports as well as those on the Atlantic, Gulf, and Pacific coasts. This recognition of the Great Lakes position as a seacoast has given rise to the frequent references to the Great Lakes as America's Fourth Seacoast."

The Act authorized the establishment of a Tax Deferred Capital Construction Fund for the purpose of providing replacement vessels, additional vessels or reconstructed vessels in

Wives of cabinet members are greeted at Massena by Administrator David W. Oberlin as they disembark for a day's inspection of the St. Lawrence Seaway. Touring with the group was Transportation Secretary John A. Volpe.

Ice operations on the St. Lawrence Seaway are observed by White House Fellows who line the gate at Eisenhower lock. Pictured are Administrator David W. Oberlin, Pierce A. Pierre, Stuart A. Taylor, Glen Wegner, HEW, Miss Pastora Esperanza San Juan, Victor Sparrow, Michael H. Armacost, Charles M. McArthur, Robert Sansone, Hudson Drake, George Wills, C. Nelson Doarney, W. Landis Jones, George Shepard, Judge Dickson, F. Dana Payne.

Lake Carriers' Trimble.

the lakes. The mere establishment of this fund served as an incentive to lake carriers to modernize their fleets, setting the stage for the revitalization of the U.S. Great Lakes shipping industry.

It meant that shipyards could apply for subsidies in the construction of merchant fleet vessels. It meant that vessel operators—American flag vessels—could qualify for U.S. subsidies in the transporting of cargoes overseas. And once the American flag vessels were in the Lakes, the system would at last have a chance to handle Departments of Defense and Agriculture cargoes.

The Merchant Marine Act of 1970 also meant that the Maritime Administration would be required to treat the Great Lakes the same as it treated the other three coastal ranges.

Since passage of the Wiley Dondero Bill, which provided for the actual construction of the Seaway—nearly a dozen years ago—there hadn't been such good news for the Seaway.

By 1975, although the Merchant Marine Act of 1970 had stipulated that the Great Lakes should be granted the same status as the other coasts by the U.S. Maritime Administration, MarAd Administrator Robert J. Blackwell had not put a regional office on the Lakes.

The maritime affairs of the Great Lakes could be better handled from Washington, he said:

"I have carefully considered the establishment of a Great Lakes regional office. I believe that the Maritime Administration's objectives in promoting domestic and foreign shipping on the Great Lakes can be best accomplished by the existing centralized structure within the Office of Domestic Shipping in Washington . . . the establishment, at this time, of a Great Lakes regional office would be impractical."

Unsatisfied with this kind of thinking, the Lake Carriers Association wrote to Sen. William W. Proxmire, head of the Great Lakes Conference of Senators.

"We have long felt that a Maritime Administration Regional Office for the lakes, similar to that of the Coast Guard and Corps of Engineers, would help make MarAd more responsive to lake shipping problems."

Paul E. Trimble, President of the Lake Carriers noted, ". . . The rationale for the lake regional office was outlined in a paper submitted to MarAd . . . Even though that letter has not yet been answered, similar letters from members of Congress to MarAd have elicited a non-responsive negative response."

In the interim, John Blatnik, the inveterate Seaway champion from Duluth, had retired from office for reasons of health, and had actively supported the candidacy of his young administrative assistant, James Oberstar, for his seat.

Oberstar had picked up his former boss' vigorous enthusiasm for the Seaway. One of the freshman Congressman's first acts in the new Congress was to introduce HR 3, a bill specifically directing MarAd to open that Great Lakes office. It passed. In mid-1975 an office was established for MarAd in Cleveland, with a marketing office earmarked for Detroit.

Later on, the overnight emphasis on energy conservation, arising out of the fuel shortages of the mid-seventies, was to create a further awareness of the Seaway.

The value of water transportation as an energy-efficient mode arose out of energy utilization studies at government laboratories at Oak Ridge. The following comparisons were made in terms of energy consumption per ton/miles of fuel consumed.

Airplanes . . . . 37 ton miles per gallon
Trucks . . . . 38 ton miles per gallon
Railroads . . . . 200 ton miles per gallon
Waterways . . . . . . 250 ton miles per gallon
Pipelines . . . . 300 ton miles per gallon

The Lake Carriers' Association indicated that a supership such as the Stewart J. Cort can carry 647 tons of cargo one mile on a gallon of diesel fuel. They stated also that the performance of Great Lakes vessels, in general, well exceeds the Oak Ridge statistics.

Statistics soon emerged to translate these figures into even more meaningful terms:

Considering the movement of 15 million tons of iron ore from Head-of-the-Lakes to lower Lake Michigan, a comparison of transportation modes indicated that it would take 200 ships, carrying 50,000 tons per trip, to transport the cargo. It would similarly take 2,308 trains consisting of 100 65-ton capacity freight cars (with a per-trip capacity of 6,500 tons), or 600,394 trucks (dual or tandem axle, with trailer) with a 25 ton per trip capacity.

The movement of the 15 million tons of ore would encompass a distance of 800 miles by water, 465 by rail or 490 by highway. Fuel consumption on a ton-mile/gallon basis indicated that it would take 24 million gallons of fuel to transport the 15 million tons of ore via the Great Lakes water route, 35 million gallons by rail and 123 million gallons by highway.

The saving of water over rail was cited as 11,000,000 gallons, with nearly 100,000,000 gallons of fuel saved in shipping by water rather than by highway.

Hugh Scott, by now the nation's Senate Republican Minority Leader, reported to a Washington Round-up of The Council of Lake Erie Ports, "As the Department of Transportation matures and picks up the broad-scope functions which it ultimately must perform, we should see a coordinated effort on the part of the Maritime Administration and the Department of Transportation that will assure the growth of the Seaway in overseas traffic.

"As I see it, some of the benefits to be realized from the growth of waterborne traffic include:

"—A reprieve for the rail systems of the northeast and midwest regions at a time when they face the uncertainties of bankruptcy and reorganization.

"—A savings in transportation costs for American commodities and goods that must compete in overseas markets.

"—Reduced inflationary pressures.

"—An improvement in our balance of trade position resulting from increased overseas sales.

"—Sizeable increases in the number of jobs for a labor force known world-wide for its productivity and efficiency.

"—The conservation of huge quantities of fossil fuels derived from making greater use of the energy efficient waterways, and finally

"—The provision of a complementary and supplementary mode of transportation to go along with our rail, highway, pipeline and air networks for a truly efficient system.

"These are just a few of the reasons why I share with so many the dedicated belief that the Great Lakes-St. Lawrence Seaway System must grow. And I understand that a significant increase in overseas traffic can be achieved without penalizing the other transportation modes, carriers or seacoasts."

Upon the eve of his retirement, "Mr. Seaway," John Blatnik, introduced legislation to take the Seaway Administrator's job out of the political arena—to make it immune to the politics of the administration in power. He proposed a seven year term for the administrator rather than a presidentially concurrent term.

The legislation passed, and Blatnik and virtually everyone else involved with the Seaway in Washington and in the hinterland of the Great Lakes began to sound the drums for Oberlin to be named to the new seven year term.

Within hours after President Gerald Ford placed Oberlin's name in nomination for a newly-authorized appointment, the Great Lakes Task Force sounded its approval to legislative leaders in Washington. Speaking for the Task Force, John A. McWilliam, Chairman of the Great Lakes group and former President of the American Association of Port Authorities told legislators that "The Great Lakes Task Force, consisting of major Great Lakes ports, labor unions, shipping interests, as well as the eight Great Lakes states as represented by the Great Lakes Commission, wishes to express its deep appreciation and thanks to you for your personal efforts which have led to the nomination by President Ford of D. W. Oberlin to fill the seven year term as administrator of the St. Lawrence Seaway Development Corporation.

"Confirmation by the Senate of the appointment will enable Mr. Oberlin to vigorously continue his exceptional record of imaginative leadership and courageous action on behalf of the Great Lakes."

The telegram went to all members of the Great Lakes Conference of Senators, as well as a number of Congressmen who responded to the Great Lakes recommendation of Oberlin for the post.

In February, 1976, Oberlin was confirmed by the Senate and a week later, in early March, he was sworn in—the first administrator who could work for the system without a political Sword of Damocles laying over his head.

In October, 1975, a long-sought amendment was added to Section 809 (a) of the Merchant Marine Act of 1936, which required that at least 10% of MarAd funds be allocated to serve the foreign trade requirements of all four seacoasts of the United States. Known as the Mondale Amendment, the provision was seen as an effective means of promoting added foreign trade for the Great Lakes-St. Lawrence Seaway system.

A widely quoted editorial in *Seaway Review* summed up the newly forming Seaway situation:

"A maturity has come to the Great Lakes, born out of a lot of things that have happened here and in Washington and overseas . . .

"New legislation guarantees us a Seaway administration with sufficient tenure to do a job without concern for the political whims of the hour. Other legislation guarantees us a regional Maritime Administration office, a long-sought goal of the Task Force and others. We have a three-year labor contract that works for the Lakes as well as the union membership. We have a solution to the pilotage issue. Not to mention success upon success for the winter navigation demonstration effort—such as a 12-month season on the upper four lakes and the earliest opening in history for the Seaway.

"And, of course, the advent of American flag service in the lakes, arising initially out of the Lykes Bros. decision to establish a regular service to the Mediterranean area, has got to be one of the best things that has happened here in years. Now, Export-Import Bank sponsored cargoes, PL 480 (USDA) cargoes, U.S.-Soviet Agreement cargoes and the much-sought-after DOD cargoes from which the Seaway was heretofore precluded, can flow from Great Lakes ports.

"All these things were going for us.

"Sure, there are a lot of problems—economic and otherwise — to which we must address ourselves. But the fact remains that today, the Great Lakes-Seaway System has more going for it than ever before."

The Council of Lake Erie Ports and the Great Lakes Task Force, together speaking for virtually every organization on the Great Lakes—labor, industry, ports, the eight Great Lakes states themselves—awarded a special citation to Oberlin for his innovative leadership. In it, they said:

"With an absence of controversy and with a minimum of personal recognition, David W. Oberlin has refined the administration of the St. Lawrence Seaway Development Corporation to make it more responsive to the needs and desires of Seaway users and more effective in translating these into policies and action.

"The St. Lawrence Development Corporation is, in fact, no longer caretaker of a public work but an instrument for forming and carrying our national policy in the operation of an international waterway vital to the economic well-being of the Great Lakes area."

And that says it all.

Prime Minister Pierre Trudeau of Canada and U.S. President Richard M. Nixon meet to reenact dedication of Seaway 10 years later, in 1969.

Seaway Tenth Anniversary: President Nixon, Prime Minister Trudeau and their wives greet crowds during bi-national celebration at Seaway lock.

Corps of Engineers, Coast Guard, and Environmental officials initiate pump out procedures from the sunken Sidney F. Smith, on facing page. Frenzied activity takes place to eliminate environmental dangers from oil spill as ship hangs precariously off an under water shelf in the St. Clair River, where the Guard Cutter Acacia stands by the wreckage. At right, passengers scramble to safety on the overturned hull of the passenger ship Easland which sank in 1915 at Chicago, taking 1,000 people to their deaths. The overloaded cruise ship, which turned over as it cast off, was taking members of the Western Electric Co. on an excursion. Over 3,000 were aboard. Chicago newspaper below tells of sinking. Note that photo at right was taken only moments after picture appearing in Chicago Daily News.

Sinkings in the Seaway System are rare. It was well over 10 years since the Seaway opened that the first ship, a laker called the Eastcliffe Hall, sank in Lake St. Lawrence. The ship, carrying pig iron, sunk in 55 feet of water minutes after it struck a reef. The ship carried nine men, including its captain, to their deaths.

Seaway traffic was briefly halted to keep transiting ships from interfering with rescue operation conducted by SLSDC and Ontario Provincial Police.

In 1973 the bulk carrier Sidney F. Smith, Jr., sank in 35 feet of water in the St. Clair River near Detroit after a collision with a grain carrier. Some 49,000 gallons of heavy Bunker C fuel oil were removed from the ship, which hung precariously off an underwater shelf. The vessel developed a three-foot crack just forward of amidships as the result of gravity and wave action. Officials stopped traffic, fearing the ship would split in half and sink in the deep channel.

As many as 35 ships were backed up as salvage crews, Coast Guard, Corps of Engineers and environmental agencies from both the United States and Canada worked to avoid both a serious oil spill and a further sinking of the ship. Ships were allowed to pass slowly—at about nine knots—to minimize the wave action against the hull of the 500-ft. ship. There were no injuries.

The worst disaster in Great Lakes history took place in July, 1915, when an overloaded passenger ship, the Eastland, turned over at Chicago with a loss of 835 people. Bound for Michigan City, Ind., the ship had moved slowly away from the pier, when it began to roll from one side to the other, as first slowly, then moire repidly and with increased momentum, until she keeled over completely in 19 feet of water. The passengers below deck in saloon and cabins never had a chance.

12

And Then There's the Future

The U.S. Army Corps of Engineers—watchdog of all the waterways of the nation—has advised Congress that it would be wise to call upon the International Joint Commission, that intreped bi-national organization which recommended the construction of the St. Lawrence Seaway in the first place, to look into the possibility of further work on the system.

Specifically, the Corps has investigated the value of constructing an All-American Canal to run between Lake Erie and Lake Ontario as an alternative to the Canadian-owned Welland Canal.

The study has revealed that by 1990 traffic in the Seaway system will be so great that a permanent jam-up will occur at the Welland, damaging the economy of all 19 states in the Great Lakes hinterland. The study did not consider the similar impact on the Canadian economy. The $1.9 million study investigated types of locks to be constructed, a path for the new canal and the economic advisability of construction. The Corps indicated that while it would be economically unsound for the U.S. to construct the canal based upon U.S. shipping needs alone, it admittedly did not consider the immense amount of Canadian traffic that moves through the system.

A computer simuation analysis of the Welland by the Corps determined that without major structural improvements, it would become a bottleneck of immense proportions for the Great Lakes.

Not only will there be too many vessels to handle, but also, if the trend in fleet composition continues, traffic will be further constrained by the fact that many vessels will be too large to pass through the existing canal, the study also showed.

"If this occurs, the Great Lakes region will lose a significant amount of future waterborne commerce, necessitating the use of more costly means of distributing bulk and general cargo commodities."

The Corps report emphasized that a proposed new canal would not replace the Welland, but rather would "serve as a parallel canal to provide additional capacity."

A harbor would be built on Lake Ontario at the entrance of the new canal. The waterway would become an integral part of the Great Lakes-St. Lawrence Seaway System permitting domestic shipping between the Great Lakes the transit of ocean going ships from the North Atlantic to ports throughout the system.

The canal would have a minimum bottom width of 600 feet to meet standards for two-way traffic, and a minimum depth of 30 feet. The locks, designed by the Corps, would be 110 feet wide by 1,200 feet between gates and would permit passage of a maximum size vessel of approximately 105 feet by 1,000 feet.

Four locks with a lift of 80 feet each are proposed for the overland section. Surge basins would be required to minimize surges in the channel (also in the overland section) caused by rapid displacement of large volumes of water during filling and emptying the locks. Also in the overland section the establishment of the waterway would necessitate the relocation of approximately 300 residences, 12 roads, four railroads and 20 utilities. The Niagara River section would require major bridge and railroad replacements.

The cost of the canal was estimated (at 1972 prices) at $2,327,600,000. The figure breaks down like this:

Lands and Damages........	25,000,000
Relocations	582,000,000
Locks.....................	690,000,000
Channels and Canals......	529,000,000
Recreation Facilities	10,000,000
Lake Ontario Harbor	163,000,000
Operation and Maintenance Facilities	16,800,000
Total Construction Cost.....	$2,015,800,000
Engineering and Design	60,500,000
Supervision and Administration	161,300,000
Total Project First Cost................	$2,237,600,000

The All-American Waterway would provide additional capacity sufficient to meet the pro-

jected waterborne traffic demand between Lake Erie and Lake Ontario through the 2040 decade.

In addition to the transportation savings, the proposed canal would also provide immediate savings to shippers through reduced traffic delays. The Great Lakes system would benefit by increased efficiency in maintenance and in insurance against accidents or failure that would require a temporary shutdown which happened at the close of the 1974 season when a ship hit a bridge abutment, forcing the closing of the Welland Canal and therefore the entire Seaway route, for many days.

"If the trend in navigation season extension continues, parallel canals become even more important in efficient maintenance scheduling," the Corps has noted. "In emergency situations, the positions of both countries would be enhanced by having a larger capacity and two canals in operation. The canal would (also) stimulate the development of the region around it as a result of benefits to the local economy through the construction and operation and maintenance of the waterway."

Another Corps of Engineers study has looked to the advisability of twinning, or doubl-

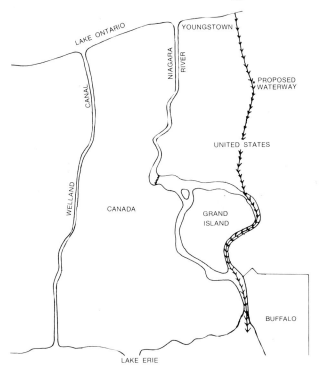

Map shows proposed route for All-American Canal.

ing, the locks in the Seaway system—putting new, larger locks alongside the old ones. The locks could permit ships to pass through both locks at the same location going in the same or opposite direction.

The locks are at present normally limited to 30,000 ton vessels. Installation of the larger locks would allow 45,000 ton vessels to use the system.

While the length and width of the new locks would be considerably greater than the present locks, the depth of the channel would not be made lower than 30 feet.

The channel in the Seaway now runs from 27 to 30 feet.

The proposed locks would be 1,200 feet long and 110 feet wide (Rep. Blatnik noted that he wanted the original Seaway locks to be "at least 100 feet wide and 1,000 feet long" when he co-authored the original Seaway bill.)

Meanwhile, Canada too has been looking into the possibility of both twinning her locks and of improving the Welland Canal. A billion dollar project to build Canadian superlocks has been under investigation since before 1970. It includes the construction of 1,200 ft. locks in the area of the existing St. Lawrence locks, and includes a project of constructing four new superlocks between Thorold, Ontario and Lake Ontario to replace the seven existing Welland locks. The new Welland Locks would also be over 1200 feet in length, and would be capable of a lift of 180 feet each.

The Welland, on an average, handles about 10 million more tons of bulk commodities than does the Montreal-Ontario section of the Seaway, due largely to the movement of coal and iron ore from the upper lakes to Lake Ontario ports.

This extra tonnage, plus the prospects for the continued growth of the system, had led Canadians to be somewhat anxious about the continued efficiency of the Welland. There are today less than 40 ships out of a total Great Lakes fleet of some 300 lakers and shallow draft canalers that can fit into the Welland locks. Maximum size which the locks can handle is only 730 feet length and 27 feet width, with cargo loads of up to a maximum of 28,000 tons.

While the Canadians have not moved in the direction of the new locks, they have approved the expropriation of some 2,200 acres of land at an estimated cost of some $7 million to the east of the existing Welland locks. In 1966 Canada also authorized its Seaway Authority to expropriate about 4,000 acres of land on the eastern edge of the City of Welland a proposed Welland by-pass which was completed in 1974. (See Chapter IV.)

These improvements, today so badly needed to allow the Seaway to achieve its full capacity, will come about because of the nature of the system, and because of the nature of the men who believe in it and who fight for it. Thanks to the vision of the early Seaway pioneers and the courage of the men who have since fought for each inch of progress, the future of the system is as secure as its inheritance.

The Seaway, born in strain and duress, whose growth was so unspectacular and whose maturity came along only after a decade of

Lakers at midwestern steel mills.

1817 sketch shows artist's concept of locking along the Erie Canal.

indifferent operation—that waterway system is here, it works, and it is good for the nation. It is finally becoming a viable force in the nation's transportation program. And that, really, is all its originators, proponents and champions ever wanted for it in the first place.

But what of the legend? What of the heroic efforts to win the right for the Seaway to exist? What of the Herculean struggle to make the earth surrender to the needs of man, to give up its land-locked domain of the Great Lakes? How can this greatest of engineering feats achieve the inspiring status of a Suez or Panama?

What will it take to put the St. Lawrence Seaway on the lips of school children, or television news commentators? What will it take to let the homemaker know that much of her food, her furniture, her transportation, her home—indeed, many aspects of her very way of life—come to her up the stair-stepped locks and through the narrow channels of the St. Lawrence Seaway?

It probably will take someone to write a ballad about it, the way someone wrote about John Henry and immortalized the western movement of the railroads. It probably will take someone to create a folk hero, such as Paul Bunyan. It will take, at any rate, the focus of public attention upon the Seaway to give it the national recognition it deserves. But most of all, it probably will take the passage of time to permit the integrity and the wisdom of perspective.

The platitudes that we live by are mostly born of hindsight. Vision is predominantly rear-view. And history, as we all know, is written by the victors. And so, the proper placement of the Seaway in both history and legend must come in due course when those forces which write the histories and create the legends get to the era, and look for its champions.

In the meantime, perhaps a volume such as this will get things started.

When you take into account the overall inland United States waterway system (see map), it is apparent that today a water route exists from New Orleans to Montreal, tying in the west as far as Tulsa and the east as far as Memphis. While drafts vary from as little as six feet in the River to 27-ft in the Great Lakes channels, the waterway system is there to be used and can well be used with either a "lighter" or a feeder service. This working trade route most certainly will be considered one day when U.S. government transportation experts or the Corps of Engineers pay more specific attention to the needs of waterborne commerce, of inland navigation, and of the fuel-efficient movement of the bulk cargo of the nation.

It does not take much vision to imagine a great water network connecting such separate parts of the nation as Omaha, Minneapolis-St. Paul, Chatanooga, Louisville, Pittsburgh, Cincinnati, New Orleans and Tulsa with Detroit, Cleveland, Duluth, Toronto and Montreal.

This national resource has never been fully explored, let alone exploited. Very possibly, at some distant date, this national water transportation system could be the subject for a battle as vociferous and as difficult as the fight for the Seaway itself.

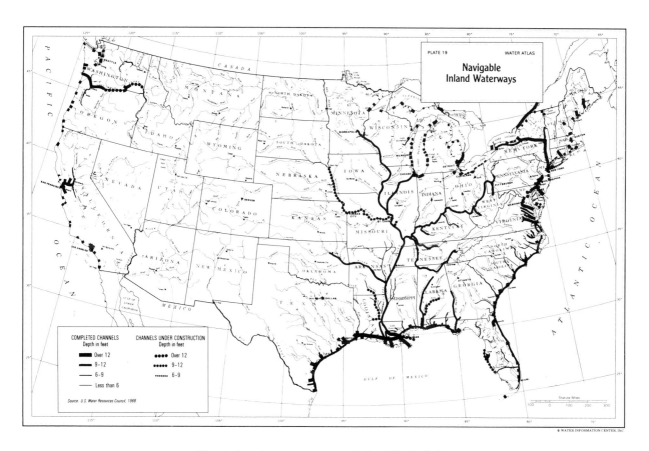

The inland waterways of the United States.

PHOTO CREDITS

Note: Photo credits are shown below in terms of the author's source for photograph, rather than a specific photographer who might have taken it, except where the photographer was known and specifically named.

Stuart Abbey 2, 7, 12, 13, 15, 20, 23, 24, 25, 28, 29, 35, 36, 38, 71, 73, 80, 85, 87, 93, 94, 95, 98, 101, 102, 105, 107, 108, 114, 136, 137, 143, 153, 154, 155, 163, 165, 166, 168, 180, 204 ★ St. Lawrence Seaway Development Corporation 4-5, 14, 20, 21, 37, 40, 43, 51, 54, 55, 58, 60, 65, 67, 68, 74, 90, 91, 92, 98, 100, 103, 104, 142, 148, 160, 161, 162, 170, 173, 176, 180, 182, 184, 185, 191, 194, 196, 197 ★ St. Lawrence Authority 40, 50, 60, 78, 85, 89, 99, 100 ★ Hans van der Aa 8, 48, 60, 61, 62, 63 ★ Department of Army 44, 46, 68, 69, 70, 80, 81, 83, 162 ★ Howard Weiss 72, 109, 110 ★ National Oceanographic Atmospheric Association 16 ★ Detroit Harbor Terminals 30, 117, 195 ★ New York Department of Commerce 61, 88 ★ Ontario Hydro 52, 53, 57 ★ Power Authority, State of New York 56, 58 ★ Wartsila Ship Yards 37, 159 ★ National Film Board (Canada) 59 ★ Blatnik Archives 32, 34, 39, 40, 44, 45, 193 ★ Imperial Oil 79 ★ U.S. Postal Department 75 ★ Dwight Welden 82 ★ American Airlines 84 ★ Port of Toronto 87, 126, 129, 131 ★ Cleveland Cayahoga County Port Authority 106, 121, 126, 127, 171, 186 ★ Seaway Port of Duluth 111, 118, 178 ★ Port of Toledo 116, 123, 126, 141, 147 ★ Port of Chicago 119 ★ Port of Indiana 120 ★ Port of Ashtabula 123 ★ Port of Buffalo 124 ★ Port of Rochester 125 ★ Port of Ogdensburg 125 ★ Port of Erie 127 ★ Port of Milwaukee 127, 130, 132 ★ Great Lakes Maritime Academy, Northwestern Michigan University 135 ★ Port of Hamilton 132 ★ Port of Green Bay 134 ★ Great Lakes & European Line Inc. 110 ★ International Association of Great Lakes Ports 140 ★ Cary Brick 144 ★ R. Robertson 145 ★ U.S. Coast Guard 150, 162 ★ U.S. Navy 151 ★ U.S. Department of Transportation 152, 179, 192, 194 ★ Chicago Maritime Council 152 ★ Dow Chemical Company 163 ★ University of Michigan 183 ★ The White House 187, 190 ★ State of Michigan 202 ★ Water Information Centre 206

Dust jacket: front, Stuart Abbey, inside rear flap, Jon Choate

INDEX

DISTANCES BETWEEN PORTS ON THE GREAT LAKES

	Port Arthur	Duluth	Ashland	Houghton	Marquette	Sault Ste. Marie	Escanaba	Green Bay	Milwaukee	Chicago	Muskegon	Alpena	Bay City	Collingwood	Port Huron	Detroit	Toledo	Cleveland	Erie	Buffalo	Port Colborne	Rochester	Oswego	Toronto	Kingston	Ogdensburg	Montreal
Port Arthur		169	143	101	149	237	428	487	540	596	510	356	439	461	471	525	572	618	691	751	737	839	883	785	899	951	1,053
Duluth	195		81	156	227	342	534	593	646	702	616	462	545	567	577	631	679	724	797	857	843	945	989	891	1,005	1,057	1,159
Ashland	164	93		114	185	303	494	554	607	663	576	422	505	528	537	591	638	685	757	818	803	905	949	851	965	1,017	1,119
Houghton	116	179	131		73	192	382	442	495	552	465	311	394	417	426	480	527	573	646	706	692	793	838	740	853	905	1,008
Marquette	171	261	213	84		138	328	388	441	498	412	258	340	363	373	427	474	520	593	653	639	740	785	686	800	852	955
Sault Ste. Marie	273	394	349	221	159		190	250	303	360	273	119	202	225	234	288	335	381	454	514	500	601	646	547	661	713	816
Escanaba	492	614	568	440	378	219		88	175	238	157	212	295	327	376	381	428	474	547	607	593	694	739	640	754	806	909
Green Bay	560	682	637	509	447	288	101		156	222	149	272	354	386	387	441	487	534	607	667	653	754	799	700	814	866	969
Milwaukee	621	743	698	570	508	349	201	180		74	70	325	407	439	440	494	541	587	660	720	706	807	852	753	867	919	1,022
Chicago	686	808	763	635	573	414	274	255	85		99	381	464	495	496	550	598	643	716	776	762	864	908	810	924	976	1,078
Muskegon	587	709	663	535	474	314	181	171	80	114		295	377	409	409	463	510	556	629	690	675	777	821	723	837	889	992
Alpena	410	532	486	358	297	137	244	313	374	439	339		101	161	136	190	237	283	356	416	402	504	548	450	564	616	719
Bay City	505	627	581	453	391	232	339	407	468	534	434	116		223	141	195	242	288	361	421	407	508	553	454	568	620	723
Collingwood	531	653	608	480	418	259	376	444	505	570	471	185	257		224	278	325	371	444	504	490	592	636	538	652	704	806
Port Huron	542	664	618	490	429	269	376	507	506	571		157	162	258		54	101	148	220	280	266	368	412	314	428	480	582
Detroit	604	726	680	552	491	331	438	561	568	633	533	219	224	320	62		47	94	166	227	212	314	358	260	374	426	528
Toledo	658	781	734	606	545	385	492	614	622	688	587	273	278	374	116	54		83	161	221	206	308	352	254	368	420	522
Cleveland	711	833	788	659	598	438	545	698	675	740	640	326	331	427	170	108	96		89	153	139	241	285	187	301	353	455
Erie	795	917	871	743	682	522	629	767	759	824	724	410	415	511	253	191	185	102		68	65	158	202	104	218	270	373
Buffalo	864	986	941	813	751	592	699	751	828	893	794	479	484	580	322	261	254	176	78		22	139	165	67	181	233	335
Port Colborne	848	970	924	796	735	575	682	868	812	877	777	463	468	564	306	244	237	160	65	22		102	146	48	162	214	316
Rochester	965	1,087	1,041	913	852	692	799	919	929	994	894	580	585	681	423	361	354	277	182	139	117		51	83	77	128	231
Oswego	903	1,025	979	964	903	743	850	806	980	1,045	945	631	636	732	474	412	405	328	233	190	168	59		126		94	197
Toronto	1,016	1,138	1,110	851	790	630	737	937	867	932	882	518	523	619	361	299	292	215	120	77	55	83	126		161	190	294
Kingston	1,034	1,156	1,156	982	921	761	868	997	998	1,063	963	649	654	750	492	430	423	346	251	208	186	89	55	161		55	158
Ogdensburg	1,094	1,216	1,170	1,042	981	821	928		1,058	1,123	1,023	709	714	810	552	490	483	406	311	268	246	147	108	219	63		120
Montreal	1,053	1,159	1,119	1,008	955	816	909	1,115	1,176	1,241	1,141	719	723	806	670	608	601	524	429	386	364	266	227	338	182	120	

Distances in Dark Type are in Nautical Miles.
Distances in Light Type are in Statute Miles.
The Great Lakes area is connected with the Atlantic Ocean area by the Junction Point Montreal.